A Student's Guide to

F. Scott
Fitzgerald

UNDERSTANDING LITERATURE

A Student's Guide to

F. SCOTT FITZGERALD

Eva Weisbrod

Enslow Publishers, Inc.

40 Industrial Road   PO Box 38
Box 398   Aldershot
Berkeley Heights, NJ 07922   Hants GU12 6BP
USA   UK

http://www.enslow.com

Copyright © 2004 by Eva Weisbrod

All rights reserved.

No part of this book may be reproduced by any means
without the written permission of the publisher.

Library of Congress Cataloging-in-Publication Data

Weisbrod, Eva.
    A student's guide to F. Scott Fitzgerald / Eva Weisbrod.
       p. cm. — (Understanding literature)
    Summary: An examination of the life and work of American author F. Scott
Fitzgerald, whose novel, "The Great Gatsby," is often called "The Great
American Novel."
    Includes bibliographical references (p.) and index.
    ISBN 0-7660-2202-1
    1. Fitzgerald, F. Scott (Francis Scott), 1896-1940—Juvenile literature.
2. Authors, American—20th century—Biography—Juvenile literature.
[1. Fitzgerald, F. Scott (Francis Scott), 1896-1940. 2. Authors, American.]
I. Title. II. Series.
PS3511.I9Z914   2004
813'.52—dc21

                          2003011358

Printed in the United States of America

10 9 8 7 6 5 4 3 2 1

To Our Readers:
We have done our best to make sure all Internet Addresses in this book were active
and appropriate when we went to press. However, the author and the publisher
have no control over and assume no liability for the material available on those
Internet sites or on other Web sites they may link to. Any comments or suggestions
can be sent by e-mail to comments@enslow.com or to the address on the back
cover.

Illustration Credits: Library of Congress, pp. 27, 48; Princeton
University Library, pp. 10, 19, 21, 24, 29, 37, 116, 138.

Cover Illustration: Princeton University Library (inset); Corel
Corporation/ Hemera Technologies, Inc.; Library of Congress (background
objects).

CONTENTS

THE JAZZ AGE

"I want to give a
*really **bad** party."*

This sentence could sum up the era of F. Scott Fitzgerald. The speaker is Dick Diver, the main character in Fitzgerald's novel *Tender Is The Night*. Diver, like many of the characters populating Fitzgerald's novels and short stories, is preoccupied with the desire to have a good time. Diver explains to his wife: "I want to give a party where there's a brawl and seductions and people going home with their feelings hurt and women passed out in the cabinet de toilette. You wait and see."[1]

Fitzgerald dubbed the 1920s the "Jazz Age," after the new kind of music that was being played in clubs across the United States.[2] During this time, young people seemed determined to break away from the mores and tastes of previous generations. As they began listening to jazz, they also started new trends in fashion. Some young women started wearing short skirts cut above the knees when, just ten years earlier, it would have been scandalous if a woman exposed her ankle in public. Despite the enactment of prohibition in 1920, people also continued to drink alcohol, and many smoked cigarettes.

Prohibition was a period in U.S. history that began with the passing of the Eighteenth Amendment in 1920, which outlawed the sale of alcoholic beverages. Many people ignored the ban however, and contin- ued to drink illegal beverages supplied by bootleggers. The Eighteenth Amendment was abolished in 1933 and remains the only amendment to the U.S. Constitution ever to be repealed.

The new breed of girl was called a "flapper." Flappers had short hair, cut in a style called a "bob." Long locks piled high on womens' heads were out of fashion. After all, you couldn't have fun if you were worrying about your hair falling down—and people wanted to have fun. Fitzgerald, more than any other writer, vividly captured this spirit of the Jazz Age in his prose. As author E. L. Doctorow wrote: "[of those] hero-novelists who came of age in the '20s . . . the Jazz Age kid, our own Fitzgerald. . . . was the most natural and unforced. . . . he wrote nearer to the societal heart than [any] of his august contemporaries."[3]

COMMON THEMES

Fitzgerald's writing deals primarily with themes of wealth, youth, and beauty. Fitzgerald often treated these themes with a two-pronged approach, offering two opposing views of each subject. As Fitzgerald himself once put it: "The test of a first-rate intelligence is the ability to hold two opposed ideas in the mind at the same time, and still retain the ability to function."[4]

Fitzgerald's writings, therefore, often illustrate the beautiful trappings of wealth versus the moral bankruptcy lying beneath those trappings; the glory of the American Dream in principle, versus the dream's ugly failures in reality; the brilliance and beauty of youth versus their inevitable loss as one grows older. More broadly, these themes can be viewed as idealism versus realism; romanticism versus cynicism.

Fitzgerald would repeat these primary themes throughout his literary career, but with each successive story or novel, the work grew in depth and quality. He once observed: "Mostly, we authors must repeat ourselves—that's the truth. We have two or three great and moving experiences in our lives—experiences so great and moving that it doesn't seem at the time that anyone else has been so caught up and pounded and dazzled and astonished and beaten

The chronicler of the "Jazz Age," F. Scott Fitzgerald.

and broken and rescued and illuminated and rewarded and humbled in just that way ever before. . . . Then we learn our trade, well or less well, and we tell our two or three stories—each time in a new disguise—maybe ten times, maybe a hundred, as long as people will listen."[5]

COMMON LITERARY DEVICES

Fitzgerald made use of many different literary devices throughout his works, but his most commonly used device was symbolism—usually sweeping and romantic in nature, and often quite poetic.

Perhaps the strongest (and possibly the most famous) example of Fitzgerald's use of symbolism is the billboard of T. J. Eckleburg in *The Great Gatsby*, where the eyes of the billboard are meant to symbolize the eyes of God, watching the "valley of ashes" (the modern world) from above. This is just one

literary device—*A formula in writing for producing a certain effect, such as a figure of speech (a metaphor, for example), a narrative style (first person, third person, etc.), or a plot mechanism (such as a flashback).*

symbolism—*The device of using one person or thing to represent or suggest another person or thing.*

11

of the more obvious illustrations of symbolism in Fitzgerald's work; other symbols may not be as readily apparent.

NARRATIVE STYLE

Fitzgerald wrote almost exclusively in the third-person. He only deviated from this with *The Great Gatsby*, which was narrated in the first-person (by the character of Nick Carraway). Perhaps it is no coincidence that *Gatsby* is considered the author's greatest work. Despite this, Fitzgerald would not write in the first-person again in any of his other novels.

LANGUAGE

Although it may not be obvious to the casual reader, language was an important tool for Fitzgerald. Different types of American English are utilized throughout his works. These styles include Midwestern, Southern, and East Coast speech, and even some ethnic dialects (as with Meyer Wolfsheim, for example, in *The Great Gatsby*, and his exaggerated pronunciation of "Oxford" as "Oggsford").

Fitzgerald often used dialect as an indication of social class, with those characters possessing East Coast (or British) accents usually coming from wealthier backgrounds. In other cases, language indicated a character's honor and integrity. In *Gatsby*, for example, Tom Buchanan often speaks in rough language despite his wealthy upbringing. Conversely, Jay Gatsby uses polite and mannered language, usually speaking with a British accent, despite his Midwestern, working-class background.

CHARACTER TYPES

F. Scott Fitzgerald's characters were usually young and wealthy American men and women, many of whom possessed artistic leanings. Their tastes and styles reflected those of the Jazz Age almost perfectly. As critic Malcolm Cowley noted: "More than any other writer of these times, Fitzgerald had the sense of living in history. He tried hard to catch the color of every passing year, its distinctive slang, its dance steps, its songs . . . its favorite quarterbacks, and the sorts of clothes and emotions its people wore."[6]

More often than not, Fitzgerald modeled his characters after himself, his family, and his friends. The male protagonists in his fiction are

protagonist—*The leading character or hero of a literary work.*

nearly all based, at least in part, on Fitzgerald himself. His first love, Ginevra King, probably served as the inspiration for Isabelle in *This Side of Paradise* and, quite possibly, Jordan Baker in *The Great Gatsby*.

13

Fitzgerald's wife, Zelda, is widely considered the inspiration for *Gatsby*'s Daisy Buchanan, as well as Nicole Diver in *Tender Is the Night*.

This autobiographical aspect of F. Scott Fitzgerald's work was most appropriate since—for many readers and society-watchers of the 1920s—Fitzgerald, together with his wife, Zelda, personified the era.

ART IMITATES LIFE

Scott and Zelda Fitzgerald were infamous for their wild antics. Their idea of fun, it seemed, was to wreak havoc wherever they happened to be. On one occasion, the two were kicked out of the Biltmore Hotel in Manhattan for disturbing the other guests. Instead of just quietly moving into another hotel, they checked into the Commodore (another luxury hotel), and celebrated their eviction from the Biltmore by spinning in the Commodore's revolving doors for half an hour.

Another time, Zelda bribed a taxi driver to let her ride on the taxi's hood because she wanted to see how it felt to be a hood ornament. Writer Dorothy Parker was among those who witnessed Zelda's bizarre cab ride down New York's Fifth Avenue. "They [Scott and Zelda] did both look as though they had just stepped out of the sun," Parker later said of the Fitzgeralds. "Their youth was striking. Everyone wanted to meet [them]."[7]

Scott and Zelda Fitzgerald's most famous stunt, perhaps, was the time they decided to take a bath in public. Because they were in a good mood, the Fitzgeralds leapt into the fountain at Union Square in New York. They did it many times, in case anyone failed to get the point. Scott and Zelda were exhibitionists, apparently determined to live their lives as the ultimate joyride.

Dorothy Parker (1893–1967) was a poet, short-story writer, and literary critic who was famous for her quick, dry wit. During the 1920s, she was one of the "Algonquin Round Table"—a group of famous writers who met regularly at the Algonquin Hotel in New York City.

AN AGE OF DISILLUSIONMENT

The Fitzgeralds may have seemed to live perfect, carefree lives, bouncing from one party to the next, but what appeared to be fun and games on the surface was, in truth, a means of escape. Ultimately, the Fitzgeralds' excesses reflected a deep-seated disillusionment with the modern world. Despite the end of World War I, a booming national economy, and all of the advances being made in medicine and technology, the problems of the United States—and of the entire world, really—seemed to be growing more complex, not less. Spiritual truth, in particular, seemed to remain especially elusive for Fitzgerald and his contemporaries. As Fitzgerald wrote in *This Side of Paradise*, his generation had "grown up to find all gods dead, all wars fought, [and] all faiths in man shaken."[8]

The above passage is just one example of how masterfully F. Scott Fitzgerald portrayed the disillusionment of an era in his writing. Drawing upon many of his own life experiences as source material for his work, he beautifully and accurately captured all of his pains, along with his pleasures.

Today, Fitzgerald's novels, stories, and essays are nearly all recognized as American classics. His novel *The Great Gatsby* is often described as the "Great American Novel." With *The Great Gatsby*, *This Side of Paradise*, *The Beautiful and Damned*, and *Tender Is the Night* to his credit, F. Scott Fitzgerald stands as one of the finest writers America has ever produced.

A
ROMANTIC
EGOTIST

F Scott Fitzgerald was born on September 24, 1896, in St. Paul, Minnesota, to Edward and Mollie Fitzgerald. Scott's birth was a source of hope for the Fitzgeralds because their two older daughters, Mary and Louise—only one and three years old—died while Mollie was pregnant with Scott. As a result, the Fitzgeralds were obsessed with Scott's well-being. Although Mollie and Edward Fitzgerald would have another daughter, Annabel, in 1901, Scott always felt that his mother never really recovered from the deaths of her older daughters.

Fitzgerald's family environment exposed him to many social backgrounds. His full name, Francis Scott Key Fitzgerald, hints at his heritage: he was named after Francis Scott Key, to whom he was related on his father's side. Key was a lawyer best known today for having composed the U.S. national anthem, "The Star Spangled Banner."

Mollie Fitzgerald's family were Irish immigrants. Her grandfather was a successful grocer, and when he died he left the family a large inheritance. Although his mother's side of the family was wealthier, Edward Fitzgerald's family had more social clout. The young Scott Fitzgerald became a great observer of social nuance, and the conflicts between societal classes would become a theme in nearly all of his works.

Edward Fitzgerald was a businessman who never lived up to his potential—or his wife's expectations. In 1898 the Fitzgeralds moved from Minnesota to New York, living in Buffalo and Syracuse. Edward was following business opportunities, and while the family was excited about the move, they were disappointed when the businesses did not prosper. No doubt, his father's failures in business also had a profound effect on the themes of F. Scott Fitzgerald's fiction.

GROWING UP

Early on, Scott Fitzgerald craved acceptance and popularity. At school, the most popular boys were the ones who excelled at sports, so Scott tried his hand at the various games his classmates played. Success as an athlete eluded him, however, as did popularity with his fellow students.

F. Scott Fitzgerald as young child with his father, Edward Fitzgerald.

The Fitzgeralds returned to Minnesota in 1908. Upon their return, Scott was sent to the private St. Paul Academy for three years. While there, his interest in literature took root. Jeffrey Meyers notes in his biography of Fitzgerald that during these years Scott went to bookstores and memorized the book titles so he could name-drop. He did not read the books; he just liked to talk as though he had.[1]

As an author, Scott believed he could win the fame he craved. While at St. Paul, he developed from a school newspaper reporter into a fiction writer. He wrote stories for the school paper and plays for the drama club. Scott's ambitious first story was "The Mystery of the Raymond Mortgage." Strangely enough, the story did not feature one word about a mortgage.[2]

Despite the genius he would later display in his writings, Fitzgerald was not a gifted student as a young man and he did not do well at the St. Paul Academy.[3] In 1911 his frustrated parents shipped him to a strict Catholic boarding school, the Newman School, in Hackensack, New Jersey. Fitzgerald was pleased at this, believing that an Eastern education would offer him advantages over boys out West. But once again, Fitzgerald struggled both academically and socially.

Fitzgerald did meet one person at the Newman

F. Scott Fitzgerald on his hobbyhorse at age two.

School who would become very important to him.
Father Cyril Sigourney Webster Fay taught at
Newman and led religious services. He was an enthu-
siastic reader—a fan of the Decadents (a school of
late nineteenth-century European and British writers, including Oscar Wilde and J.K. Huysmans).[4]
Father Fay befriended Fitzgerald and introduced him
to some of these experimental writers. With Father
Fay's encouragement, Fitzgerald would enroll in
college in 1913.

A POOR BOY IN A RICH MAN'S WORLD

With an inheritance from his maternal grandmother,
Fitzgerald could afford a private college and avoid
what he considered the great embarrassment of
attending a public institution. When considering colleges, Fitzgerald quickly set his sights on Princeton
University. He had trouble getting into the presti-
gious school at first, but was eventually accepted.[5]
There was one particular group at Princeton that
Fitzgerald wanted to join: the Triangle Club. Triangle
was famous for its comedic plays, which were staged
on campus and taken on national tours during vacation
breaks. No other college had anything like it, and it

was one of the main reasons Fitzgerald had been so determined to get into Princeton.

Fitzgerald quickly realized that he was not up to the social standard of his fellow classmates, many of whom came from very wealthy backgrounds. Many of these boys had gone to prep school together and already knew each other. This made it difficult for Fitzgerald to make friends at first. In 1938, he reminisced about his early college days: "A poor boy in a rich town; a poor boy in a rich boy's school; a poor boy in a rich man's club at Princeton."[6]

At Princeton, Fitzgerald again tried to be a star athlete and failed. His attempts at literary fame, however, were more successful. He became friends with two other members of Triangle: Edmund "Bunny" Wilson and John Peale Bishop, both of whom would eventually become well-known American men of letters. Their friendships were significant and would remain strong throughout Fitzgerald's life.

FIRST LOVE, FIRST HEARTBREAK

Unfortunately for Fitzgerald, Wilson and Bishop were practically his only friends at Princeton. In fact, Fitzgerald did not have much of a social life at all until he met a young woman back at home during

F. Scott Fitzgerald at age eleven, 1907.

the Christmas break of 1914. At a dance in St. Paul, Fitzgerald met Ginevra King, a beautiful and wealthy Chicago debutante. She was Fitzgerald's first infatuation, the first of many women Fitzgerald knew who embodied all the things he could not have. The doomed romance taught him important lessons about love and money. Fitzgerald later wrote that the reasons he failed to win King were that he "didn't have the top two things—great animal magnetism or money."[7]

Despite this, Fitzgerald pursued King for the better part of a year. The relationship ended in 1916, at which point King's father supposedly told Fitzgerald that "poor boys shouldn't think of marrying rich girls."[8] In 1918, Ginevra King married a wealthy aviator. Fitzgerald found out when he received her wedding announcement in the mail. Fitzgerald saved a photo of King, along with a newspaper clip about her wedding, in a scrapbook. At the bottom of this page in his scrapbook, Fitzgerald scribbled, "The End of a Once Poignant Story."[9]

Fitzgerald's failed romance with King would color his ideas about women and love for the rest of his life. In his writing, Fitzgerald began to model his characters on himself and King, who represented the wonderful, almost-within-reach, but ultimately unattainable woman. At Princeton, he worked on a book based on his experiences. He titled it *The Romantic Egotist*.

DEVELOPING HIS FIRST NOVEL

Fitzgerald attended classes and toyed with homework but mostly he worked on his own writing. *The Romantic Egotist* became his only interest. Naturally, his grades suffered as a result. Fitzgerald was flunking out when he contracted malaria (then a common malady). Princeton University grudgingly wrote him a reference letter stating that Fitzgerald had withdrawn from college in good standing, but it was not quite true. When he re-enrolled months later, after regaining his health, his grades failed to improve.

All of Fitzgerald's attention was on *The Romantic Egotist*, which was both autobiographical and polished fantasy. He offered the manuscript to a professor, writer Christian Gauss. Gauss' opinion was that it was not very good yet, but that it had potential. Fitzgerald rewrote the book, determined to perfect it. He was sure the book would change his life.

LIFE IN THE ARMY

Meanwhile, Fitzgerald's academic record was so poor, he opted to leave school without graduating and enter the army. Leaving college without a diploma would be less of an embarrassment after he had earned respect in the military, Fitzgerald

26

believed. He imagined himself as a sort of poet-soldier—a common fantasy during World War I. Fitzgerald joined the 45th Infantry in March 1918 and worked on his book in his free time.

Once he had completely rewritten the novel, Fitzgerald sent it to a writer friend, Shane Leslie. Leslie was impressed, and sent the manuscript to the publisher Charles Scribner's. An editor there named Maxwell Perkins read it and saw great promise in it. It was not yet good enough to publish, Perkins said, but could someday be something very special.

The Army stationed Fitzgerald on Long Island

The Fitzgerald family home on Summit Avenue in St. Paul, Minnesota.

and, later, in Montgomery, Alabama. He was in Alabama from June 1918 until February 1919. While there, he attended a number of parties. At a country club in the summer of 1918 he met a young woman named Zelda Sayre, a recent high school graduate. Pretty and sharp-witted, Fitzgerald took to her right away.

World War I began in June of 1914 with the assassination of Archduke Francis Ferdinand of Austria. This caused Austria to declare war on Serbia—the nation Austria believed to be behind the assassination. Other European nations quickly chose sides and the conflict grew rapidly. The U.S. entered the war in 1917, after German subs began sinking U.S. ships. While each side expected a quick victory, the war lasted more than four years and took the lives of nearly 10 million people.

THE LOVE OF HIS LIFE

Zelda was born on July 24, 1900, to Minnie and Anthony Sayre. Anthony Sayre was a successful lawyer who became a judge as a young man. The artistically inclined Minnie was an attentive mother to Zelda and her four siblings. On her maternal side, Zelda's family had a history of emotional instability. Fitzgerald was unaware of this. He found the flamboyant Zelda's many quirks attractive, and grew quite infatuated with her.

A young Zelda Sayre, pictured here at about the time
she first met F. Scott Fitzgerald.

The war ended on November 11, 1918, and Fitzgerald was released from service in February 1919. James Mellow's biography of Fitzgerald stresses that Fitzgerald was disappointed in himself for not having seen combat, viewing it as a serious personal failure.[10] Fitzgerald biographer Matthew Bruccoli notes that Fitzgerald made up various cover stories to justify why he never "got over" (went overseas, to Europe, to fight).[11] Later Fitzgerald would write an essay about his "failed" army service.

In January 1919, Fitzgerald's mentor, Father Fay, died during the flu epidemic which killed millions worldwide. Fitzgerald mourned but the gap left by Father Fay's death was very quickly filled by Zelda Sayre.

Zelda Sayre was flirtatious and liked to shock people for fun. Over the course of their courtship, she and Fitzgerald fought and made up, over and over again. In springtime 1919, the two decided to marry. She insisted—perversely, Fitzgerald felt—that they not wed until he was financially stable. The Sayre family strongly supported Zelda's position in this regard. The two continued to bicker over the issue and, by June 1919, Zelda had broken off the engagement. Still, Fitzgerald remained confident. He felt that the way to win her back was to write the most successful novel ever published. He moved to New York and dedicated himself to becoming an author.

STRUGGLES TO SUCCEED

Fitzgerald sent stories to magazines, and though the short-story market was massive, his work was rejected. In those days writers could become wealthy selling stories to magazines such as *The Saturday Evening Post* and *Scribner's*. At one point, Fitzgerald had 122 rejection slips stuck on the walls of his New York apartment.[12] Frustrated, Fitzgerald moved back to Minnesota and lived with his family while he worked on his fiction. Fitzgerald's writing style began to develop during this time.

Fitzgerald was still not earning a salary to satisfy Zelda Sayre or himself, however. Sayre wrote to Fitzgerald, "There's nothing in all the world I want but you—and your precious love. All the material things are nothing. I'd just hate to live a sordid, colorless existence, because you'd soon love me less—and less."[13] Trying to improve his fortunes, Fitzgerald moved back to New York City, where an old friend from Princeton, Edmund Wilson, found him a job writing advertising copy. All the while, he continued to write and submit stories to magazines.

A SUCCESSFUL DEBUT

In 1919, at Max Perkins' recommendation, Fitzgerald retitled *The Romantic Egotist* as *This Side of Paradise.* Fitzgerald took the new title from a poem by World War I poet Rupert Brooke. The book was published on March 26, 1920, and was an immediate best seller. His friends were impressed, though all agreed with Fitzgerald's surprisingly humble observation that much of the book was not very good. It was ambitious, however, using several different writing forms to tell the story of Amory Blaine.

THIS SIDE OF PARADISE

This Side of Paradise focuses on the adolescence and young adulthood of one Amory Blaine. Amory aspires to a lifestyle to which he was not born. Middle-class but not very wealthy, bright but not truly intellectual, he observes his classmates and envies them. He falls in love with girls who like him but who never take him seriously because they know Amory will not be able to support them financially in the fashion they expect. This basic plot is one that Fitzgerald would revisit numerous times in his writing career.

THE PROTAGONIST

The novel's original title, *The Romantic Egotist*, had captured Fitzgerald's feelings about his life just before and after leaving Princeton. Amory's life parallels Fitzgerald's, with some embellishment. He is born out West and moves to the East Coast during his teenage years. Amory goes to college, has a few complicated and disastrous affairs (the Ginevra King influence is considerable), and the book ends with his young adulthood nearly over but unresolved. Fitzgerald described *This Side of Paradise* as "a novel about flappers written for philosophers." The apt description was later used in advertisements for the book.[1]

THEMES OF *THIS SIDE OF PARADISE*

The novel belongs to a literary genre called the *bildungsroman* (German for "coming-of-age novel").

The term describes a story depicting the growing up of its protagonist. The protagonist is followed through his or her emotional, educational, and spiritual development over the course of the narrative. A *bildungsroman* usually ends as the character reaches young adulthood.[2]

Fitzgerald analyzed Amory Blaine's family relationships, using the novel as a way of exorcising some of his demons about his own family. Amory's smothering, well-intentioned mother is partly a caricature of Mollie Fitzgerald. Despite Fitzgerald's issues with his own mother, most of the character's traits are ones Fitzgerald would have found highly desirable in a mother.[3] Fitzgerald often returned to the theme of the dominating mother, and would, in the mid-1920s, start (and then abandon) a project titled "The Boy Who Killed His Mother."

epistolary—*Contained or carried on by written correspondence; pertaining to or consisting of letters. An epistolary novel is a novel mainly consisting of letters written by the characters.*

This Side of Paradise is a mixture of styles, consisting of various short chapters. Fitzgerald was ambitious and showed off, writing the novel in prose, poetry, playscript, and epistolary forms. The book's pomposity fits the character of Amory Blaine nicely. Fitzgerald's lustful imagination finds life in Amory;

the romances Fitzgerald is too shy to have, Amory dives into with enthusiasm.

COMMERCIAL SUCCESS

The book received glowing reviews and sold very well. Its literary ambitions were not intimidating to readers of the day, who were probably more drawn to the notorious content. The book talked frankly about sex more than other novels of the time. One chapter bore the titillating title "Petting." Biographers and literary critics often note today that while the passages about sex and romance are tame by current standards, today's reader must remember that when the book was written, a kiss was practically a promise of engagement. Fitzgerald's book became a bible to young readers, a touchstone, as *The Catcher in the Rye* and *Less Than Zero* would be for readers in decades to come.

What shocked readers of *This Side of Paradise* was not its actual descriptions of sex, but more its attitude toward the subject. The characters are not promiscuous, but they engage in activity that ten years before would have been shocking. The shortening of the girls' skirts was just a start.

Amory's three girlfriends are all thoroughly modern. Ginevra King was the inspiration for at least one and possibly more of these characters. Isabelle,

Rosalind, and Eleanor are all charmingly mercenary in their approach to courtship, and sometimes a little bit crazy. (Eleanor's emotional problems in particular are based on Zelda's.) Amory seems unaffected by romantic failure. When the novel ends, Amory appears to have learned almost nothing about life. Spottily educated, entirely dependent on inherited money and professionally unskilled, he claims high-mindedness. The reader, however, sees otherwise.

juvenilia—*A literary work written and designed for a young audience; also, works produced in a writer's youth.*

This Side of Paradise was the best selling of Fitzgerald's books during his lifetime. It is a fun, entertaining read, but now ranks as a relatively minor work. Often regarded as juvenilia, it is worthwhile because the reader senses talent and style which show great potential. Fitzgerald's editor, Maxwell Perkins, said as much at the time.

A LIFE CHANGED

Fitzgerald wrote advertising copy for the Barron Collier agency while trying to sell his fiction. He was not successful in advertising; his best-known line was "We Keep You Clean In Muscatine," from an ad for a cleaning company in Iowa. When *This Side of Paradise* was published, everything changed for

F. Scott and Zelda Fitzgerald were wed on April 3, 1920, in New York.

Fitzgerald. Once the book was published, he quickly sold stories to several magazines. Soon he was a very highly paid writer, and Zelda Sayre was impressed.

Scott Fitzgerald married Zelda Sayre on April 3, 1920. Their parents did not attend the Manhattan wedding. They were breaking out on their own, in New York, far from their Midwestern and Southern families. In the beginning of their marriage, the Fitzgeralds enjoyed Scott's tremendous success. They were celebrities, living well on the money Scott's novel had earned. They lived in hotels and attended an endless stream of parties.

SELECTED SHORT STORIES

America in the 1920s was as in love with its celebrities as it is today. Scott and Zelda Fitzgerald were among the most famous celebrities of the era. They charmed paparazzi and newspaper columnists. They were seen everywhere, moving from one party to another, with the parties never seeming to end.

Scott was writing at a furious pace and was being paid handsomely for his work. *This Side of Paradise* had earned him more money than he had imagined possible, and because of the novel's success, magazines were also paying him very well. In advertising, he made $90 a month. In 1919, his fiction earned him $879 (nearly equaling his earnings from the ad agency Barron Collier), and by 1920, he would earn $18,850 from writing—a staggering sum at the time.[1] Stories he wrote quickly and carelessly, which he often characterized as trash, sold for hundreds and even thousands of dollars. Some of his best-known stories, however, were written during this period. "The Ice Palace," published by *The Saturday Evening Post* in May 1920, just before the Fitzgeralds married, is an excellent example of Fitzgerald's work at the time.

"The Ice Palace"

"The Ice Palace" is a sketch of a popular, Southern girl. The story describes how the charmingly lazy Sally Carrol, much admired in her Georgia hometown, plans to marry a Northerner. Her friends disapprove of nice Harry Bellamy, but she loves him and does not care what her friends think.

Harry invites Sally Carrol to come North, to meet his friends and family and go to a Winter Carnival. She is excited, but is disappointed on arrival. The North is another culture, another climate, and she is unprepared for it. Not only is she literally very cold, but she finds the people strange and unfriendly.

As she and Harry ride home from the train station, Sally Carrol has her first experience of things feeling amiss. Seeing some children sledding, she turns to Harry and says it looks like fun. She asks if they can ride on sleds, too. Harry, not appreciating Sally Carrol's idea of a good time, admonishes her that sledding is for kids. Harry's role as the adult figure in the relationship is made clear by virtue of Sally Carrol's wanting to play the way children do.

The Bellamy's house further frustrates Sally Carrol. The house is big and well-furnished, but it strikes her as being too new. It feels unfriendly to her. Fitzgerald's nuanced eye describes the house's library, breaking down the class and economic differences Sally Carrol feels:

> It was a large room with a Madonna over the fireplace and rows upon rows of books in covers of light gold and dark gold and shiny red. [The] books looked as though they had been read—some—and Sally Carrol had an instantaneous vision of the battered old library at home.[2]

The newly bought, barely touched books; the over-attention to neatness and cleanliness, while perfectly attractive, leave Harry's house cold and unlived-in to Sally Carrol. She bravely tries to charm her hosts, and join their social circle, but it is not easy. Her sleepy Southern ways are too ingrained. She cannot get used to the North. When Harry asks her, early in her visit, if she is happy to be there, she answers enthusiastically that she is "awful glad," but at the same time, she feels as if she is "acting a part."[3]

Sally Carrol spends a lot of time with the Bellamys and their friends. She always finds that the only people she likes are the men who have a connection to the South. The women all strike her as old-fashioned and cold. Harry's mother clearly disapproves of her, and will not even call her by her proper name:

> She called Sally Carrol "Sally," and could not be persuaded that the double name was anything more than a tedious ridiculous nickname. To Sally Carrol this shortening of her name was like presenting her to the public half clothed.[4]

Sally Carrol keeps trying to win people over, but it never quite works. Sally Carrol and Harry quarrel about cultural differences but they make up, determined that they will not quarrel after they are married.

They visit the massive ice palace at Winter Carnival, and everyone there is amazed by its beauty. Only Sally Carrol finds the coldness unpleasant, and she tries to be game about it, but she becomes lost. She hallucinates a visit from a woman buried in the cemetery near her home and thinks she is going to freeze to death.

After hours of hunting for Sally Carrol, some guests find her and bring her back to safety. All Sally Carrol can say is that she wants to go home, tomorrow. She will not marry Harry. The story closes with a scene almost identical to its beginning, back in Georgia, with Sally Carrol eating a green peach.

LITERARY DEVICES IN "THE ICE PALACE"

When the story opens, Sally Carrol Happer sits at a window in her house eating an apple. The apple is a Biblical allusion. It evokes the apple eaten by Adam and Eve in the Garden of Eden. Eating the apple allowed Adam and Eve to know things God did not want them to know. As "The Ice Palace" goes on, Sally Carrol will see things she does not want to see and discover she only wants to go home.

allusion—*An incidental mention of something, either directly or by implication, designed to hint at some deeper meaning.*

The geographical climates described in the story are symbolic. The climates of the U.S. North and the South are generally the opposite of one another—one is typically cool and the other warm. Historically, the North and South fought a bloody civil war. The war ended in 1865, but Fitzgerald seems to imply that the North and South still have not fully reunited at the time of the story. Sally's retreat to Georgia at story's end, therefore, is no act of cowardice—it is the recognition of knowing where she really belongs.

FORBIDDEN FRUIT

Fitzgerald's use of geography also brings to mind a parallel to the Garden of Eden in the book of Genesis in the Bible. Adam and Eve were born as natives of the Garden of Eden, but it became foreign to them after they had tasted the forbidden fruit, the apple. In the story of the Garden of Eden, Adam and Eve were at first unclothed and innocent. After eating the apple, they saw their own nakedness, and clothed themselves. The landscape and climate changed after they tasted the forbidden fruit. In Georgia, Sally Carrol would have lounged on her windowseat wearing linen dresses—but up North, she would feel naked in those clothes (as she feels when Mrs. Bellamy strips her of her second given name, and rechristens her in Northern fashion). In the cold North, she bundles up and wears mittens. To Sally Carrol, the South is her Garden of Eden. Only when she leaves it does she feel naked and cold.

Fitzgerald's symbolic use of fruit imagery is emphasized and made clearer at the end of "The Ice Palace," when Sally Carrol is at home in Georgia, eating a green peach. A green peach is unripe, of course. Sally Carrol knows that eating unripe fruit is not a good idea. She observes calmly that she is "'spectin' to die any minute." The Georgia peach is a metaphor. The peach is a symbol of the state of Georgia, where it is a major agricultural crop, and of attractive young women like Sally Carrol. (Pretty Southern girls are often described as "Georgia peaches"—beautiful, sunny, sweet, and delightful.)

> **metaphor**—*A figure of speech in which a comparison is made between two words or phrases that have no literal relationship.*

The peach-eating also serves as a metaphor for her experience up North: when she went to visit Harry Bellamy, she was an unripe peach. Now, back home, she is not the frantic and terrified girl she was in the ice palace. At home, she eats fruit she knows might make her sick, and she could not care less. She has utter faith that everything will work out fine. Up North, she feared for her life, but down South, she jokes about death, and eagerly consumes the symbol of Southern beauty—of her innocent self.

By eating an unripe peach, Sally Carrol shows that she has knowledge and self-consciousness (like Adam and Eve after they had eaten the apple). After eating an apple at the beginning of "The Ice Palace," Sally Carrol has gained awareness of the consequences of her actions, and she is unafraid of what may come. The reader may wonder what it means that she takes the risk of eating the potentially poisonous, unripe peach. One possible explanation is that Sally Carrol feels she is older and wiser and that by eating the peach she is destroying her younger self. The new Sally Carrol will be savvier than the young Sally Carrol—she will not make the same mistakes twice.

Parallels With Other Short Stories

Biblical allusions like the one in "The Ice Palace" to the book of Genesis can be found throughout much of Fitzgerald's work. A later story by Fitzgerald, "Babylon Revisited," is titled with a Biblical allusion. Babylon was an ancient city known for chaos and its citizens' degenerate behavior. To describe a place as a Babylon is to imply that it is a sinful place.

Another theme which is found in "The Ice Palace" and to which Fitzgerald returned in later works is the soulless nature of American culture—which usually results from its material greediness. In "The Ice Palace" the Northerners are materialistic and lacking personal depth (as seen in the description of the Bellamy library). The South, by comparison, is warm climatically, emotionally, and spiritually. America, chaotic with its many merging traditional and modern lifestyles, was a new Babylon. Stories like "The Ice Palace" were followed by many others, notably "May Day," which explored this theme more directly.

FITZGERALD'S WOMEN

Fitzgerald sketched women adeptly. Many of his friends in real life were women, and his affection for women is apparent in his work and his personal letters. Zelda gave birth to a daughter, Frances Scott Fitzgerald, on October 26, 1921. Fitzgerald was devoted to Scottie, as she was nicknamed. When she grew up and went away to school, Fitzgerald wrote to her frequently. He also wrote often to his sister, Annabel. His letters to them were filled with advice, most of it sound, which Fitzgerald had learned from his experiences. Teenaged Annabel got advice on how to be popular with boys. Scottie got advice on schoolwork.

"The Ice Palace," like much of Fitzgerald's fiction, draws from his personal experiences. Sally Carrol is based, at least in part, on his wife Zelda; Tarleton, Georgia, is based on Zelda's hometown of Montgomery, Alabama; and the Northern city is modeled on Fitzgerald's hometown of St. Paul. At the time he wrote the tale, Zelda had never been to St. Paul, but Fitzgerald knew how she would react to it. He believed that Zelda, just like the fictional Sally Carrol, would initially be convinced she could adapt to the Northern city, and when she found she could not, would quickly retreat back home.[5] In Sally Carrol, Fitzgerald neatly captures the prototypical

47

F. Scott and Zelda Fitzgerald on their honeymoon in 1920.

Southern belle. It is a character type Fitzgerald would revisit several times in later stories.

"BERNICE BOBS HER HAIR"

Fitzgerald continued to develop his female characters in "Bernice Bobs Her Hair." The story covers the experience of a girl, Bernice, who visits her cousin Marjorie for a month. The story was published in 1922, when bobbed or short hair was controversial. When preachers and public speakers lectured on the ills of contemporary American culture, bobbed hair was the symbol of America's moral decay. Many said that alcohol, cigarettes, and bobbed hair were the American female's unholy trinity.

"Bernice Bobs Her Hair" contrasts modern and old-fashioned character types. Marjorie is popular, with many boyfriends. Her primary interest is calculating how to get the most boys to dance with her at a party. Cousin Bernice, visiting from Wisconsin, is popular in her hometown but feels like a fish out of water in Marjorie's circle out West. Bernice does not know that her dances have all been arranged by Marjorie and that no one likes her. Marjorie complains to her mother about Bernice.[6]

Overhearing the conversation, Bernice is shocked. She cannot imagine why Marjorie's friends dislike her. Back home, she is the belle of the ball. Her parents throw parties, everyone comes, and all the boys dance with her. She has a car, and lots of attention. Bernice has modeled herself after her mother, believing in dainty femininity. Marjorie's world, in which girls kiss boys and behave wildly is completely foreign to her. Bernice wishes she could discuss her difficulties with Marjorie, but finds her cousin to be "rather cold," and not possessed of those qualities which Bernice considers "appropriately and blessedly feminine."[7]

Eventually, Bernice confronts an unapologetic Marjorie. Bernice says she will go home, since she is so unwanted, and expects Marjorie to protest—but Marjorie does not. Bernice adds that if Marjorie showed common kindness, things might be different, but Marjorie snaps at her, saying "Oh, please don't quote *Little Women!* That's out of style."[8] After Bernice cries, Marjorie agrees to take on Bernice as a charity case. If Bernice does everything Marjorie tells her to do, Bernice will find her social life transformed.

Bernice follows Marjorie's instructions. Marjorie feeds her lines to say at dances and generally tells her how to conduct herself. Eventually, she convinces Bernice to bob her hair. Bernice announces she is going to bob her hair, publicly, at a local barbershop, and she wants the boys to watch. The boys are thrilled, and everyone wants to dance with her.

Marjorie, up to this point convinced of her own beauty and popularity, becomes concerned when her own boyfriend, Warren McIntyre, shows too much interest in Bernice. Marjorie, displeased, confronts Bernice and tells her to forget Warren. Bernice is genuinely surprised by Marjorie's hostility.

─── **LITTLE WOMEN**

Little Women is a classic novel for young readers by Louisa May Alcott. Wildly popular when published and still popular today, it is a collection of tales about the March family in Massachusetts during the Civil War. The children, all girls, are brought up to be honest, forthright, and virtuous. The heroine of the book, Jo March, is an uncommonly strong female character who audaciously and presciently cuts her hair in order to sell it and earn income for the family.

After having threatened and taunted her suitors with promises to bob her hair, Bernice is finally bullied into doing it. Her long mane is cut by a confused and shocked barber at the Sevier Hotel. Bernice sits zombielike as the barber (whom she thinks of as a hangman) chops off her hair. Marjorie stands with the boys and watches with them.

> But Bernice saw nothing, heard nothing. . . .
> [T]his hair, this wonderful hair of hers, was
> going—she would never again feel its long
> voluptuous pull as it hung in a dark-brown glory

down her back. . . . she was near breaking down, and then the picture before her swam mechanically into her vision—Marjorie's mouth curling in a faint ironic smile as if to say:

"Give up and get down! You tried to buck me and I called your bluff. You see you haven't got a prayer."[9]

Bernice has met Marjorie's challenge, but loses her own character's virtue. To make matters worse, cutting her hair makes her less attractive, as evidenced by the disinterest of Warren McIntyre, who suddenly gives her the cold shoulder.

Bernice goes back to her cousin's home and runs to Marjorie's mother, who is horrified by the haircut. Not only does Bernice look awful, but the next night the girls are to attend a dance given in their honor by a woman whose pet peeve is bobbed hair. Bernice has no way of changing her appearance in time. While Marjorie's mother weeps over Bernice's haircut, Marjorie sits with her long blonde hair, smug and confident of her own success at the dance.

Bernice is livid and hatches a plan to take revenge on her cruel cousin. She packs her bags and gets ready to run to the train station before the dance. In the middle of the night, she puts her plan into action:

[Bernice] stood quietly until her eyes became accustomed to the darkness. Softly she pushed open the door to Marjorie's room. She heard the quiet, even breathing of an untroubled conscience asleep. . . . Bending over she found one of the braids of Marjorie's hair, followed it up with her hand to the point nearest the head, and then holding it a little slack so that the sleeper would feel no pull, she reached down with the shears and severed it.[10]

LITERARY DEVICES IN "BERNICE BOBS HER HAIR"

The cutting of Bernice's hair is symbolic on several levels. It shows Bernice is far more complicated than she originally appeared. Cutting her hair is a metaphor for severing ties, akin to the proverbial "cutting the apron strings," the separation of a maturing child from its mother. Cutting her hair separates her from her mother's generation and its mores. It is also a Biblical allusion, equating hair with personal strength and character, as in the story of Samson and Delilah. As with Samson, Bernice's strength is her hair, literally (it is her greatest physical asset) and symbolically (as she is a success as an old-fashioned girl and a failure as a flapper). Bernice's haircutting is ironic because it makes her, in ways she could never have desired or anticipated, like Jo March in *Little Women*. The bobbing of

irony—*The use of words to express an idea that is opposite to the words' literal meaning.*

Bernice's hair proves her even more old-fashioned, and more true to her values, than she ever dreamed. Simultaneously, she is modernized against her will. It makes her weaker and stronger at the same time. The rage Bernice feels at the end of the story gives her more strength than she ever before displayed, a twist on the Samson and Delilah story. The old Bernice might have swallowed that rage, and remained lady-like, but the new Bernice acts on her fury. Though Bernice idolized the characters of *Little Women*— modeling herself after the girls of the March family, Beth and Meg—the one she ends up most resembling

SAMSON METAPHORS

The story of Samson and Delilah, in the Old Testament, is often alluded to in literature. In modern literature, one can see it particularly in the works of Hemingway and Fitzgerald because the Jazz Age they wrote about was one in which women were cutting their hair short as they had never previously done. In the Bible, Samson, a judge in ancient Israel, is a legend for his strength. A wicked temptress, Delilah, discovers that the root of his strength is his long hair. Acting as a mercenary for the Philistines, she becomes Samson's mistress. Delilah dupes Samson into having his hair cut short, and in the process he loses his powers. The cutting of long hair has, in literary terms, become a standard symbol for the loss of special or unique powers. In Jazz Age works, a woman cutting her hair short is also often a symbol for the masculinization of that character.

is Jo, the willful, boyish, and most independent of the girls.

Fitzgerald's female characters here also fit the mold of the duality of holding two opposed ideas at once. With Marjorie and Bernice, Fitzgerald presents two women who are at once strong and weak, appealing and unappealing. The modern woman was similarly multifaceted and complex. Fitzgerald knew this well: he was married to one of the most modern women of her time.

CHAPTER 5

THE END OF INNOCENCE

In the first year of Scott and Zelda Fitzgerald's marriage, Fitzgerald sold eighteen stories and seemed unstoppable. Unfortunately, the couple's lifestyle was extremely expensive. The Fitzgeralds lived in New York hotels, always ate in restaurants, and worried only sporadically about the financial strains they brought on themselves. By the end of 1920 the Fitzgeralds were $1,600 in debt. Fitzgerald asked his publisher for an advance on future earnings.

TO MINNESOTA AND BACK AGAIN

The Fitzgeralds tried to live cheaply in St. Paul for a while, and their daughter Scottie was born there. But neither Scott nor Zelda was happy in Minnesota and they eventually moved back to New York. In 1921, they moved to Westport, Connecticut, in an effort to economize. Westport was an affluent town which enjoyed a reputation for being "arty." Many writers lived there. The Fitzgeralds had a romantic notion of living quietly productive lives in the country. The plan did not work. Parties followed them from New York to Westport, and their debts grew.

Fitzgerald's first story collection, *Flappers and Philosophers*, was published in September 1920. It contained "The Ice Palace," "Bernice Bobs Her Hair," and a number of other stories. Its publication was timed to maximize its potential as a follow-up to *This Side of Paradise*, but critics were unkind to it. Fitzgerald did not particularly mind—he was busy focusing his energies on his second novel.

THE BEAUTIFUL AND DAMNED

The Beautiful and Damned is generally read as a roman à clef. The novel is a portrait of Anthony Patch— another fictionalized Scott Fitzgerald—a young man with literary aspirations. The novel traces his life in college and right after college, when he lives in Manhattan with his college chums, wondering what he should

roman à clef—*A novel that represents historical events and characters under the guise of fiction.*

do with his life. After a few unsuccessful affairs, he meets Gloria Gilbert. She is, like the women in *This Side of Paradise* and many of the femmes fatales in Fitzgerald's stories, an amalgam of the real women in Fitzgerald's life. Gloria is beautiful, loves a good time, and will not waste her time on the wrong (i.e., poor) boys. She wants a wealthy man. Anthony is smitten.

THE CHARACTERS

In an attempt to write what he could not live, Fitzgerald made Anthony a success at Harvard University: "Curiously enough he found in senior year that he had acquired a position in his class. He learned that he was looked upon as a rather romantic figure, a scholar, a recluse, a tower of erudition. . . .

amalgam—*A combination or mixture of different elements.*

He made the Pudding. He drank—quietly and in the proper tradition. It was said of him that had he not come to college so young he might have 'done extremely well.' In 1909, when he graduated, he was only twenty years old."[1]

The gifts Fitzgerald lacked, he gave to Anthony Patch. In addition to being a Harvard graduate, Patch is wealthy, the grandson of a well-heeled social reformer (based on real-life American reformer Anthony Comstock). Coming to adulthood with every advantage, he is surprised when all his friends, except Gloria, expect him to have a career. Anthony and Gloria live a carefree existence together, biding their time until their wedding.

As it was for Zelda, the question of marriage is, for Gloria, a

ANTHONY COMSTOCK

The character Anthony Patch is actually named Anthony Comstock Patch, leaving no doubt that the reader is meant to think of the reformer, Anthony Comstock. Comstock was relentless in his efforts to cleanse the U.S. of all vices—particularly drinking, smoking, and gambling.

matter of finances. Fitzgerald's observations on money and personal wealth grow pointed in *The Beautiful and Damned*. Where his earlier works alluded to vast sums of money, this novel talks in dollar amounts. The theme of American wealth becomes dominant in the book. *The Great Gatsby* will elaborate on the matter of money and its effects on personality and behavior better than almost any other work in American fiction. But *The Beautiful and Damned* is precise in a way *The Great Gatsby* is not.

Gloria Gilbert is vain and self-centered. The things that interest Gloria are simple: she wants a tan, a good time, evenings out. She is easily bored, and admits it, proudly announcing her shallowness. Anthony Patch and his pals are charmed by her candid vacuousness and her beauty. Ultimately she wants a rich husband who will treat her as if he were a lover and not a husband. Gloria sees no conflict in that, and serenely waits for the right man and his money.

LOVE AND MONEY

Anthony falls in love with Gloria. He reluctantly admits that he will inherit millions from his grandfather, and that he has no occupation to fill his day, unlike their novelist friend Richard "Dick" Caramel. But Gloria does not see a problem:

"It seems to me," Anthony was saying earnestly, "that the position of a man with neither necessity nor ambition is unfortunate. Heaven knows it'd be pathetic of me to be sorry for myself—yet, sometimes I envy Dick. . . ."

She yawned.

"I've told you I don't know what anybody ought to do," she said ungraciously, and at her indifference his rancor was born again.

"Aren't you interested in anything except yourself?"

"Not much."[2]

The romance has its ups and downs, but Gloria realizes that Anthony never bores her, which is what she considers his most important attribute. And so they marry.

Gloria and Anthony feel invincible. They travel

around the country, visiting friends and going to parties. They are contentedly unemployed, though Gloria sometimes mentions that if she needed a job she could go to Hollywood and star in a movie. The Patches do not worry about money. They always have enough. They do not save money; it is always there, waiting to be spent. It is a rich boy's lifestyle, which Fitzgerald learned about at school. Fitzgerald's experiences watching college friends turn into businessmen, and trying to do it himself, are converted into Anthony Patch's apathy. Anthony thinks getting a normal job is beneath him.

The Patches' honeymoon experience parallels that of the Fitzgeralds', and Fitzgerald writes about it skillfully, with both humor and sorrow. Simple matters that most people would easily take care of send the Patches into chaos, such as the episode with the laundry in the chapter "The Radiant Hour," which describes the early part of the marriage. For the first months of marriage, the Patches live in hotels. One day, Anthony dresses and finds he has no clean handkerchiefs. He borrows one from Gloria, and realizes that their laundry has not been done in weeks. He opens the closet, which is filled with laundry. Anthony is angry: laundry must get sent out, and he does not see why he always does it. He says Gloria said she would take care of it this time. Gloria does not see the problem; one can always buy more hand-kerchiefs and underwear.

Mundane chores overwhelm Gloria. She is a picky eater who will not cook for herself. She always needs more pretty, clean clothes but refuses to put her laundry in a bag to be sent out. Anthony picks up the slack, but wonders why Gloria will not help at all.

The Patches dutifully attempt to economize and rent a house in Connecticut. The house in Connecticut is a ray of hope for the Patches. Anthony fantasizes that they will settle down once they are in a proper house. Gloria is unenthusiastic but joins in Anthony's fantasy. The house they find is perfect. It is a little gray Colonial house (symbolizing old-fash-ioned life). They sign a lease and they make plans: they'll join a country club. Gloria will golf. Anthony will write a book.

"A WARM, BLUE CLOAK BUTTONED WITH TINY STARS"

The color of the Patch's Connecticut house is signifi-cant. In the first descriptions of it, a realtor shows them the house in fading light, and Fitzgerald describes it as a comforting, sweet haven that "rested against a sky that was a warm blue cloak buttoned with tiny stars."[3]

The beauty of Fitzgerald's prose stands out here. Much like explaining the beauty of a particular painting or song, it is difficult to capture precisely what makes a written line or phrase beautiful. One way to is to rephrase the line and see how the effect is changed. If we were to say "it rested against a sky that was a warm blue cloak with tiny stars for buttons," we would be saying the same thing as Fitzgerald, essentially, but the effect is diminished. The line seems to lose some of its power without the verb "buttoned." It also seems to read more dramatically by climaxing with the word "stars."

We can rearrange the text further, like this: "it rested against a warm blue cloak of sky buttoned with tiny stars." But even this seemingly minor change causes the line to lose something—placing the word "sky" between the "blue cloak" and its "buttons" breaks up the metaphor, and seems to slow down the effect.

A GRAY EXISTENCE

The house's color is also significant in this passage because it is associated with Gloria's eyes, which, Fitzgerald repeatedly writes, are also gray. Gray, it seems, is the color of Gloria at her most vain. Early in the novel, her eyes are described as gray like "a cliff of soft granite." Later, she says she likes to wear gray because with gray clothes one has to wear a lot of makeup—i.e., put on a mask. The color there implies a desire for hard artificiality. Fitzgerald weaves references to gray throughout the book and each time it conveys a slightly different notion.

The Patches' first months in Connecticut are idyllic. While Gloria is still not handling the laundry and refuses to eat chicken, the couple are relaxed, and talk of having children. They summer in the gray house and winter in Anthony's old apartment in Manhattan. Their rents go up, but they renew the leases. Anthony's grandfather disapproves of their lifestyle, suggesting that Anthony go to Europe to work as a war correspondent. This excites Anthony, but not Gloria, who says if he goes to Europe, she will go to Hollywood. In the end, neither of them go anywhere, and they write apologetic letters to their would-be benefactors, explaining that they will be staying where they are.

After much consternation, Anthony takes a job as a salesman with a bond company in New York. The young man who shows him around brightly explains that education is useless in the context of the company. He says that he himself went to college, but working in business meant he had to deliberately forget a lot of the "fancy stuff" he learned in school. Anthony, appalled, quits the job. He does not see why he should give up his nights out, filling a soulless sales position by day.

He tells Gloria they will have to economize more and then discovers that Gloria, drunk, has renewed the lease on the Connecticut house. The house suddenly seems a dingy, dirty place. It is a trap, not a home. Gloria feels that the walls close in on her; the bedroom curtains, swishing in the wind, scare her.

During a crazy party, Anthony's ailing, wealthy grandfather visits unexpectedly. The anti-vice crusader finds Anthony, Gloria, and several pals extremely intoxicated. He leaves immediately. Anthony's fate is sealed. Grandfather Comstock cuts Anthony out of his will: Anthony will not inherit his grandfather's $30 million estate.

REAL-LIFE PARALLELS

Fitzgerald based the Patches' economic struggles on his own experience of earning a fortune on the sales of *This Side of Paradise* and losing it through carelessness. When he squandered all the money, he learned that restraint with personal finances was a virtue. In real life, Fitzgerald was constantly drawing up budgets and keeping elaborate ledgers to track the family's accounts, but nothing ever added up as expected.[4]

Anthony also keeps ledgers and argues with Gloria about finances.

The Fitzgeralds' lifestyle parallels the lives of the Patches, but it was not precisely their story. Fitzgerald wrote to his daughter in 1940: "Gloria was a much more trivial and vulgar person than your mother. I can't really say there was any resemblance except in the beauty and certain expressions she used, and also I naturally used many circumstantial events of our early married life. However the emphases were entirely different. We had a much better time than Anthony and Gloria had."[5]

A SEPARATION

Fitzgerald further complicated the Patches' marriage by having Anthony join the army. Anthony is shipped to the South while Gloria stays up North. She writes him letters wondering when she should visit him, and wondering if she should move to the South, too. Meanwhile, Anthony has an affair with a local young woman.

A battle over Anthony's inheritance, in dispute after his grandfather's death, is waged in letters featuring Gloria's pettiness and greed. Letters between Anthony, Gloria, and their attorney circulate for months and the case drags on. Over time, Anthony is happy Gloria is not with him. He writes to her explaining that she would be bored down South, and that she should stay in Manhattan. After Anthony begins his affair with nineteen-year-old Dorothy, he has even less interest in having Gloria around. He does not hide his marriage from Dorothy, but he does not dwell on it:

> She knew vaguely of Gloria. It gave her pain to think of it, so she imagined her to be haughty and proud and cold. She had decided that Gloria must be older than Anthony, and that there was no love between husband and wife. Sometimes she let herself dream that after the war Anthony would get a divorce and they would be married.[6]

But there is a cultural gap between Anthony and Dorothy. As passionate as their affair may be, their worlds are different, and they will never marry. Fitzgerald makes this plain in an exchange between the lovers. Dorothy naively thinks their problem is that Anthony is too poor to contemplate divorce:

> "If I had some money, darlin', I'd give ev'y bit of it to you . . . I'd like to have about fifty thousand dollars."
>
> "I suppose that'd be plenty," agreed Anthony. . . .
>
> In her letter that day Gloria had written: "I suppose if we could settle for a million it would be better to tell Mr. Haight to go ahead and settle. But it'd seem a pity."[7]

Dorothy's misunderstanding about Anthony's

situation is darkly comic. She understands very little about Gloria, and even less about money. Anthony agrees with Dorothy's wishful thoughts, to humor her. But Anthony thinks fifty thousand dollars is nothing and believes Dorothy naive for thinking otherwise.

The Patches' marriage remains intact, though unstable. When the war ends, Anthony is released from service (like Fitzgerald, without ever having seen battle) and heads home. He arrives to find Gloria at a party at the Astor Hotel, flirting with men. He dashes to her, they kiss, and for a moment they could not be happier.

FURTHER DISAPPOINTMENT

Despite their immediate joy at being reunited, Anthony and Gloria's marriage is still troubled. Gloria, in Anthony's absence, has found her power over men has diminished. Once a wildcat among housecats, she suddenly seems prim and prissy. Gloria also disapproves of Anthony's drinking and complains about his laziness. Why hasn't he nagged their lawyer about the inheritance, she asks? Why doesn't Anthony work? Finally, completely fed up with Anthony, Gloria calls the man who always said he would help her break into movies.

Gloria schedules a screen test. She auditions for a small role—the younger sister of the movie's heroine. Eventually she gets a letter saying that the movie director has viewed the screen test and feels Gloria is too old for the role. They suggest that there might be another part for her: the "very haughty rich widow."[8] The idea of playing such a role is a grave insult to Gloria, a wound from which she never recovers.

The story of the Patches ends dramatically. Dorothy appears uninvited in New York, arriving at the Patches' apartment while Gloria is out. Dorothy—still convinced of Anthony's devotion to her—has come to "save" him from his loveless marriage. Anthony is drunk and horrified to see Dorothy at the door. She throws herself at him and he kills her by hitting her with a chair. He promptly has a nervous breakdown. When Gloria returns with their friend Dick Caramel, the apartment is a shambles, and Anthony sits in a sunny patch of bedroom floor. He plays with his childhood stamp collection. Gloria barely notices any of this, as she has exciting news: The courts have awarded the Patches the thirty-million-dollar inheritance. When she tells Anthony the wonderful news, Anthony is annoyed with her for bothering him. "See here," Anthony tells her, "you two get out—now, both of you. Or else I'll tell my grandfather."[9] Anthony has obviously gone insane.

The novel ends on a luxury ocean liner. Anthony, swaddled in blankets, rests in a wheelchair, gazing at the ocean. Two vacationers gossip about him. The man says everyone knows Patch went crazy just after he won his inheritance. The woman says it is a lucky thing he has a doctor to accompany him. And they nod sagely when they discuss Gloria Patch. Gloria accompanies Anthony, but just barely. She prowls the ship in her fur coat, getting older. She was always in it for money, and once Anthony was awarded his full inheritance, she would not leave. Romantic Anthony is ultimately defeated by his own fantasies, by his wife, and by wealth.

THEMES OF *THE BEAUTIFUL AND DAMNED*

The novel is Fitzgerald's first large-scale attempt at addressing those themes that are recurrent throughout his works: the American Dream, its connection to youth and promise, and its corruption. The Patches, twisted by money, become precisely the kind of worn, washed-up, spiritually bankrupt people they said they would never be. They are ruined by their culture and their desires.

Their culture, of course, is the American way of life. The American sense of entitlement to live well, for the quality of life to always be improving, and to ever climb upward in society are notions that Fitzgerald sees as misguided. Money drives and corrupts American society. Anthony, Gloria, and Dorothy are all devoted to acquiring as much money as they can. Dorothy's dreams are modest compared to Gloria's, but Dorothy does not know that. Gloria's thirty million is equal to Dorothy's fifty thousand—to each woman, money incorrectly represents freedom.

Money is also associated with cleanliness, which is a metaphor in the book for a kind of spiritual purity. There is physical cleanliness, which is obviously a great concern to the Patches. (Anthony loves bathing in his Manhattan apartment; the concerns over clean laundry are discussed at such length that it is obvious they are significant.) But the laundry and bathing habits of the Patches are also indicative of the state of their souls. Gloria's inability to do laundry or even hand it off to a maid is indicative of her being unable to face the reality of her own corruption by greed. The notion of personal hygiene and attention to cleanliness as a symbol for corruption is driven home again at the end of the book. After being corrupted by greed, but before he has inherited his

71

money, Anthony (who was once very fastidious) is seen on the street by Dick Caramel. Caramel notes with disgust that Anthony wears a dirty shirt with frayed cuffs, something he would never have done before. Anthony has fallen so far from grace that he no longer cares about wearing clean shirts.

One interesting aspect of *The Beautiful and Damned* is Fitzgerald's double self-portrait. While Anthony Patch is an autobiographical character, one of the secondary leads, Dick Caramel, is also modeled on Fitzgerald.

Patch's Harvard pal Caramel serves as a foil, or contrast, for Patch and other Harvard classmates in the book. Caramel is an aspiring writer, mocked by his classmates for his pretensions. But he writes a best-selling book, and becomes very wealthy churning out stories for mass market magazines. This is precisely what happened to Scott Fitzgerald. Caramel is Fitzgerald's confession of disgust with himself and his career. When Patch expresses interest in writing, Caramel flatly explains to him how to market short stories, and how much magazines will pay for certain kinds of stories. He admits that most of his work is junk, but he says it is all about the money, after a certain point.

So even the high-minded, literary star, Caramel, is in it for money. There is no character in the novel who is entirely free of avarice. These people, Anthony, Gloria, and their friends, are the "beautiful people." They are the best and the brightest, the smartest and most popular, and in the end they have nothing. The $30 million Anthony inherits after years of court battles fails to bring him happiness.

SHATTERED DREAMS

The *Beautiful and Damned* was reviewed respectfully while F. Scott Fitzgerald continued to crank out stories. The Fitzgeralds' marriage, meanwhile, was growing strained. The fictional Anthony Patch may have lost his mind in *The Beautiful and Damned*, but in real life, it was Zelda Fitzgerald who was showing signs of mental illness.

In January of 1922 Zelda became pregnant. The Fitzgeralds felt having another child would be a mistake. They loved Scottie, but did not spend much time with her. Abortion was an illegal and often dangerous medical procedure, but they agreed that Zelda should have one. Between Zelda's deteriorating mental state and Scott's financial instability, the decision was an easy one for the couple. The procedure was performed in New York in March of 1922. In the future Zelda would have two more abortions, in addition to numerous medical procedures performed to aid conception.

Between publishing *This Side of Paradise* and *The*

Beautiful and Damned, Scott Fitzgerald published many stories. Their quality varied, and most were written purely for money, without serious artistic or literary intent. Still, a handful of them, like "Bernice Bobs Her Hair," are exceptional and were hardly "junk." At the time "Bernice Bobs Her Hair" was published, though, Fitzgerald agreed with such characterizations.[1] Two of his best stories from this period are "May Day" and "The Diamond as Big as the Ritz."

STYLES OF FICTION

During this period, a style of writing called naturalism was popular. The idea behind naturalism was that fiction should address real life problems, particularly political and social woes. This contrasted with the romanticized, glossy stories for which Fitzgerald was famous. Naturalistic writers wanted to solve problems, to raise public consciousness of the poor and uneducated American underclass. Writers such as John Dos Passos, Theodore Dreiser, and Stephen Crane wrote naturalistic fiction, and hold respected positions in the American literary canon today.

The naturalistic mode did not come easily to Fitzgerald. Nevertheless, he tried his hand at it, and touches of naturalism can be found throughout his work. Fitzgerald's attitude toward some characters' feelings about money show naturalistic tendencies, and his political leanings would keep part of his work attached to naturalism. "May Day" is his best example of the genre and it is one of his darker short stories.

"MAY DAY"

"May Day" tracks the downfall of several young people in New York City at the end of World War I. At the story's beginning, in 1919, the city is rejoicing, as soldiers coming home are making merry all over the city. In the midst of this, a recent Yale graduate named Gordon is in dire straits. A gifted artist who has squandered his opportunities, he is penniless. A girlfriend is threatening him, insisting he give her several hundred dollars he does not have.

Gordon decides to visit a college friend, Philip Dean, vacationing in Manhattan. Dean is a successful businessman, from a well-off family, in New York to celebrate the end of the war with the rest of their classmates. They plan a party at Delmonico's. Dean sees that Gordon is in bad shape and will hit him up for money, and he is annoyed. Dean is comfortable, but not fabulously wealthy. He resents Gordon's casualness about other people's money. He tells Gordon that he should be more careful; if he were cautious with women and alcohol, he would not get in trouble.

> "That's easy for you to say," began Gordon, his eyes narrowing. "You've got all the money in the world."
>
> "I most certainly have not. My family keeps darn close tab on what I spend. Just because I have a little leeway I have to be extra careful not to abuse it."[2]

Philip's financial savvy is enviable. Gordon represents all the young men of Fitzgerald's ilk, who had potential and wasted it.

Fitzgerald then introduces two opposites of Gordon and Philip. They are soldiers, Carrol Key and Gus Rose. Fitzgerald neatly condenses their lives: "They were ugly, ill-nourished, devoid of all except the very lowest form of intelligence, and without even that animal exuberance that in itself brings color into life; they were lately vermin-ridden, cold, and hungry . . . they were poor, friendless."[3]

Discharged from the service, Gus and Carrol have one goal: to get drunk. Liquor is hard to come by (sale to soldiers was illegal), so they devise a plan. They will find Carrol's brother, George, who is a waiter in town. He will be able to sneak them a bottle or two. The hunt for George leads them to his current place of employment, Delmonico's.

The Yale graduates cross paths with the former soldiers. The party spills out of Delmonico's, with Gus and Carrol sharing a bottle with one of the Yale men. A young woman with the Yale party, Edith Bradin, leads the group a few blocks away to visit her brother, Bartholomew, at his office. Bartholomew edits a local socialist newspaper. An office sign gets the visitors' attention. The Yalies, with former soldiers Gus and Carrol leading them, storm the office. Edith panics. Bartholomew tries to convince his attackers to calm down, explaining that he is not rich, he is not German, and he is not their enemy. But the scene is a madhouse. In the middle of everything, Carrol jumps out a window and Bartholomew is severely beaten. The police show up, but it is too late to save Carrol.

socialism—*A theory of social organization in which property, land, and means of production are communally owned rather than individually owned.*

The morning after the party and the brawl, Philip Dean continues drinking with a classmate, Peter. They stagger around the city in search of breakfast and champagne. Meanwhile, Gordon sits in his shabby hotel room. The room, in unfashionable Chelsea, holds nothing for him—it smells of old cigarette smoke and old booze. Feeling hopeless, Gordon commits suicide.

THE DICHOTOMY

The story focuses primarily on two classes of people: the rich and the poor. One man from each class dies in the story, and the man in the middle, who tries to bridge the two worlds—Bartholomew—takes a beating. The characters who turn to suicide appear to have been spiritually broken by their failure to attain financial success. The drunken Yalies, who are completely unaffected by the scuffle, appear almost soulless, aspiring to no deeper goals, it seems, than getting drunk.

Literary critic Edwin Fussell sums up the seeming dichotomy of Fitzgerald's work as quests and/or seductions. Fussell describes the quests as being searches for romantic wonder—or, perhaps more specifically, the American Dream. The goal of these "quests" are all the alluring surface elements of youth, pleasure, and money. Oftentimes, Fitzgerald's characters will find themselves "seduced" by these surface elements and lose sight of the original romantic ideal.

dichotomy—*A division into two contradictory parts. In logic, a term used to describe the division of an idea in two, resulting in two new, opposite ideas.*

The characters most easily seduced are those that lack the introspective qualities that might protect or save them.

This is the tragedy of the American Dream for

Fitzgerald: that it seems to emphasize material reward. In so doing, it encourages hedonism and rejects spirituality. In "May Day," Philip Dean and the other Yalies—all of whom have enough money to live comfortably—do not seem to possess much in the way of character or soul. Philip never asks the kind of spiritual questions asked by characters such as Gordon and Bartholomew. It takes a certain sort of person to wonder what makes life worth living. The spiritual and the hedonistic cannot coexist in one mind, according to Fitzgerald—therefore, the characters here fall into either one category or the other.

hedonism—*A devotion to personal pleasure as a way of life; the doctrine that pleasure or happiness is the highest good.*

Gordon sees that his own quest will be fruitless. Like so many other Fitzgerald characters, he comes to realize that eternal youth is impossible, that the pleasure of young love is fleeting, and that money usually leads to moral decay. He also understands that he has lost everything and has nothing left. Ultimately, he chooses death over living with nothing. The most sensitive character in the tale, Bartholomew, suffers bodily harm in the fracas but survives. He appears as the most sensible and spiritually aware character. The reader senses that he will move on from the episode and still lead a full life.

In his essay "Fitzgerald's Brave New World,"

Fussell characterizes Fitzgerald's depiction of the lives of modern American youths as tragedies. Fussell makes a convincing argument that Fitzgerald's ideal America would have been more old-fashioned. The "new world" of the 1920s was— despite its flash and glitter—fundamentally unattractive to Fitzgerald.[4]

NEW WORLD VERSUS OLD

Fussell strengthens the case for his ideas regarding Fitzgerald's view of the modern world by noting the reference in "May Day" to Christopher Columbus, the explorer credited with discovering North America. Toward the end of the story, as the drunken revelers eat breakfast in a restaurant, they notice the sunrise:

> The great plate-glass front had turned to a deep dreamy blue, the color of a Maxfield Parrish moonlight—a blue that seemed to press close upon the pane as if to crowd its way into the restaurant. Dawn had come up in Columbus Circle, magical, breathless dawn, silhouetting the great statue of the immortal Christopher, and mingling in a curious and uncanny manner with the fading yellow electric light inside.[5]

The statue of Columbus watches over the party-goers as they rebuild their world with the end of the war. While Columbus stands basking in the natural wonder of the sunrise, the party-goers sit in weak artificial light. It is a strong metaphor, warning readers of the dangers presented by the changing world, that the views and motives of the current generation of Americans are antithetical to those of Columbus, the original discoverer of America.

Fitzgerald's attack on American youth was heavy-handed, and it is obvious why the story did not sell quickly to *The Saturday Evening Post*. "May Day" is a story of political idealism. It is related to the kind of radicalism that many college students embrace, but it lacks a sense of optimism.

"THE DIAMOND AS BIG AS THE RITZ"

Fitzgerald attained new heights in flights of fancy with "The Diamond as Big as The Ritz," which is very different from "May Day." Where "May Day" is steeped in realism and very dark in tone, "The Diamond As Big As The Ritz" is completely fantastic and often quite humorous.

Like many of Fitzgerald's tales, it begins with a young boy shipped off to a fancy East Coast school. In this case, young John Unger's parents send him to St. Midas, a Massachusetts boarding school. The

Ungers are on top of the social heap in their small Southern town of Hades. John Unger, while fond of Hades, looks forward to being sent to school because he knows it is a privilege. His parents are excited about his journey and proud of him. They prepare him, as best they can, for his time away:

> John T. Unger was on the eve of his departure. Mrs. Unger, with maternal fatuity, packed his trunk full of linen suits and electric fans, and Mr. Unger presented his son with an asbestos pocket-book stuffed with money.[6]

The reader has to laugh at the idea of sending a boy off to a New England boarding school with linen suits and electric fans; the boy would freeze to death wearing linen, and electric fans would not be needed. Mrs. Unger means well, but does not understand her boy will be in cold New England. Mr. Unger, by comparison, knows very well what will be useful at St. Midas. A purse full of money is all the boy needs to be a success there. Mr. Unger says to his son, "Remember, you are always welcome here. . . . You can be sure, boy, that we'll keep the home fires burning."[7] Slyly, Fitzgerald conveys the corruption of values of the boy's well-intentioned parents—a reflection of the corruption of values in American society.

John Unger arrives at St. Midas and enjoys

himself there. He makes friends with a classmate named Percy Washington. When Percy invites John to come to his home out West over summer break, John accepts. Everyone knows that Percy comes from a wealthy family, and John figures a summer vacation with him will be fun.

On the train ride out West, Percy announces that his father is the richest man in the world. John is skeptical, but says he, too, is interested in wealth—particularly in jewels. Percy haughtily says that his father owns the biggest jewel in the world: a diamond as big as The Ritz-Carlton Hotel.

In Montana, the boys disembark from the train and get in a jalopy. After a short drive, the boys leave the beat-up car and enter into a splendid car made of precious metals, gems, and upholstered in silk. The trip is long and complicated. Percy explains to Unger that they are on the only five miles of land in the U.S. which has never been surveyed by the government. Unger innocently asks if the government forgot to cover the territory. Percy tells him that the government has tried to do so numerous times, but were foiled each time by the efforts of his father and grandfather. Percy tells Unger that there is only one thing the family fears—one tool that could yet find them out: "Aeroplanes."[8]

A WEALTH OF AMORALITY

Percy explains that people in airplanes would obviously be able to discover the land, and that it is a problem because the Washingtons would have to commit inconvenient murders to protect themselves. Percy admits that the thought of murder does not bother him or his father, but it upsets Percy's mother and sisters. The Washingtons take obvious and considerable pride in their greed, lacking any and all sense of morality.

At the house, John sleeps in a luxurious room and is awakened the next day to find a house slave waiting to bathe him and help him dress. The next day he learns about the house and the diamond. John learns that through a run of luck and then a string of massive, cruel acts of deception, Grandfather Washington built this estate of gems. He illegally kept slaves and murdered his own brother to protect the property.

Percy tells the story to Unger fearlessly. It never occurs to him that Unger might disapprove of Grandfather Washington's actions. None of the story strikes Percy as being unusual. Unger is too stunned by the story and awed by the wealth to offer any protest.

John meets Percy's sweet sisters, Jasmine and Kismine. John quickly falls in love with Kismine, the younger sister. Though she is proudly naive and clueless, John finds her beautiful and gentle. The one difference between the sisters is that while Jasmine has a streak of kindness in her (romantic, and naive as well, so that she would never be strong enough to do any real good with her intentions), Kismine has no charitable will in her: "Percy and Kismine seemed to have inherited the arrogant attitude in all its harsh magnificence from their father. A chaste and consistent selfishness ran like a pattern through their every idea."[9]

Kismine, in her innocence, speaks many of the most comic lines in the story. They all serve to highlight the ignorant cruelty which can result from wealth. John Unger is more than a little disgusted with her attitude, shared by Percy, Kismine, and their father, but he is so blinded by his love of Kismine and her wealth that he cannot show her the error of her thinking. When discussing their wedding, they decide to elope and avoid any public fuss. From the way Kismine talks, John assumes she disapproves of showiness, but that she also finds living beneath one's means (as was fashionable during the war years) to be just as pretentious. Her spoken view is that the rich do not understand what moderation is. John agrees with her, and they have the following

humorous exchange, with John offering the first
observation:

> "When I was visiting the Schnitzler-Murphys, the
> eldest daughter, Gwendolyn, married a man
> whose father owns half of West Virginia. She
> wrote home saying what a tough struggle she was
> carrying on his salary as a bank clerk—and then
> she ended up by saying that 'Thank God, I have
> four good maids anyhow, and that helps a little.'"
>
> "It's absurd," commented Kismine. "Think of
> the millions and millions of people in the world,
> laborers and all, who get along with only two
> maids."[10]

Kismine obviously has no idea of how most people live. John sees the absurdity in both Gwendolyn's
and Kismine's comments, but reacts negatively only
to Gwendolyn. John observes wistfully that perhaps
he and Kismine ought not to marry; that their backgrounds are too different. Kismine protests, and
unwittingly hints at unsavory incidents at the
Washington home.

John soon realizes he is one of many schoolfriend
visitors to the Washington compound, and that all
the other guests came, had a marvelous time, and
were murdered. No one leaves the Washington house
alive. John is horrified. Kismine tries to defend
her family, but cannot. John announces that
Mr. Washington will not murder him; that he will

escape during the night. Kismine plans to go with him. For all her selfishness, she loves John, and wants to be with him. John is not entirely comfortable with her love—her innocent cruelty disturbs him—but he agrees she may come along.

Their plan to run away is altered when the mountain is attacked. Airplanes are sighted flying near the house. The glory days are ending. John smartly plots escape for himself and the two girls. Kismine is thrilled by the adventure:

> . . .Then she added in a sort of childish delight: "We'll be poor, won't we? Like people in books. And I'll be an orphan and utterly free. Free and poor! What fun!"[11]

Considering Kismine's simple ideas about poverty, John orders her to grab a handful of jewels from her bureau drawer. The girls are not thinking about it, but John sees they will need money to maintain the Washington girls in the manner to which they are accustomed. He knows that a handful of gems, once sold, could provide enough money to last them a lifetime.

Scurrying to escape from death (this time at the hands of the curious airplane pilots, not Mr. Washington), John Unger witnesses an incredible sight. Mr. Washington, desperate, attempts to bribe God to save himself from disaster. He tells God that he will build a marvelous cathedral out of his huge diamond. He will build the greatest tribute to God imaginable, if only God will make everything as it was the day before, and swallow up the airplanes. Washington thinks to himself that God was made in Man's image, which means that God must have his price and that God must be someone you can bargain with.

Unger watches Mr. Washington as the skies close over him. The airplanes land. There seems to be no hope for Mr. Washington. But John and the girls are safely tucked away on the edge of a nearby valley. They can see the mountain without putting themselves in danger.

Mr. and Mrs. Washington and Percy, along with a couple of slaves, run into an underground cavern, which John presumes is an attempt to escape. Jasmine and Kismine, arriving at John's side, know better, and cry that the mountain is wired to explode. Almost instantly, the house, the Washingtons, the airplanes, and the pilots are all blown to bits.

After the dust has settled, nothing remains of the old house. Jasmine, Kismine, and John picnic in the valley, discussing their futures. John suggests that they take a look at the jewels Kismine took, so that they can get a sense of how much they will have to live on.

When Kismine empties her pocket, John is dazzled at first, and then realizes to his horror that Kismine's haul will not help them. In her rush, Kismine grabbed a handful of rhinestones, worthless paste. Kismine remembers that she traded them with a now-dead friend of Jasmine's: rhinestones for diamonds. A moment of folly has left the Washington girls with nothing to live on. They have no means, and, because of their total lack of contact with the outside world, no skills on which they can rely. Jasmine announces that, because she has always washed her own handkerchiefs, she will be able to support the three of them by taking in laundry. John says they will all have to move to Hades, and look for help from his family. He assures them that they will be able to live perfectly good, middle-class lives there, but it is clear the transition will be hard.

When Kismine asks if her father will be there, it is obvious that she has no grasp of their new reality. John tells her Mr. Washington is dead. The news does not seem to affect the girl at all.

SYMBOLS IN "THE DIAMOND AS BIG AS THE RITZ"

Many symbols in "The Diamond as Big as The Ritz" can be clearly seen. For example, John's hometown of Hades is named for the hellish underworld of Greek mythology. The metaphor is reinforced by John's father's reference to "home fires," as well as the asbestos pocketbook he gives to John. At the time this story was written, asbestos was a miraculous fireproof material, and not recognized as a health hazard as it is today. It was commonly used to make the firemen's suits, theater curtains, and house shingles. When a strong, fireproof shell or fabric was needed, asbestos was the solution. As such, it is all the more interesting that a purse full of money given to a boy in "Hades" should be made of a fireproof substance.

The St. Midas school is likewise named for a figure of Greek myth: King Midas, whose touch turned everything into gold. (In reality, of course, there is no Saint Midas.) It is at the school where John meets Percy Washington, whose family is Midas-like in their blind greed and devotion to material wealth.

Other symbols in the story are less obvious. For example, the "jewels" Kismine takes from her pocket may be seen as an example of the "Midas touch" in reverse, where the objects she touches become worthless. Perhaps more broadly, this reverse "Midas touch" symbolizes a reversal of fortune for the entire Washington family.

91

Themes of "The Diamond as Big as The Ritz"

"The Diamond as Big as The Ritz" is as much a social critique as "May Day," though the styles of the two stories are very different. The fantastic imagery in the former story is rich and luminous, as opposed to the realism of "May Day." Still, both stories make similar points about American values. In both, money is a false idol. The Washingtons never use their wealth for good purposes; they use it only to satiate their own greed. They feel their wealth justifies their terrible behavior. Fitzgerald's sense that money takes all reason away is hammered home by the story. Despite its fantastic premise, it is probably a more instructive tale than the preachier "May Day."

One Fitzgerald theme common to both stories is that of the person who has the power to help or heal, but does not—either because he deliberately decides not to, or finds himself, for one reason or another, unable to do so. The Washington family could have done great things with their wealth, but did not. Philip Dean in "May Day" has the means to help his despondent friend but will not because it would be inconvenient, or perhaps because he likes feeling superior to Gordon. (Later, Dick Diver, in *Tender Is the Night*, is a doctor who cannot heal.)

IMMORALITY VERSUS AMORALITY

The personal carelessness and heartlessness depicted in these stories is a key attribute of many of Fitzgerald's characters. The Washington children have no sense of the greater consequences of their actions—an attitude shared with their parents. None of the Washingtons have any sense that other people are hurt by the fulfillment of their petty desires. The theme is not immorality (which would be the willful commission of an evil act), but amorality—the lack of any understanding of what is good or evil, right or wrong.

Fitzgerald's work conveyed this evolving sense that modern life was not so much immoral as amoral. This was a reflection of the challenges Fitzgerald was facing in his own life, where he found himself wrestling with many difficult and complex problems.

A STORMY RELATIONSHIP

By the summer of 1924, the Fitzgeralds were living in France. At this point, they had already faced many difficulties in their marriage—excessive drinking was a problem for both Scott and Zelda; Zelda was becoming more unstable, emotionally; and the couple continued to have money problems. But now, for the first time, their relationship was on the verge of shattering. Zelda had fallen in love with another man, a famous French aviator named Edouard Jozan, and had asked Scott for a divorce. Scott refused—he still loved Zelda. Distraught over the situation, Zelda attempted suicide, but survived. Ultimately, the Fitzgeralds stayed together.

Nevertheless, the Fitzgerald marriage remained volatile. The two would fight and then make up, over and over again, driving their friends to distraction. Fitzgerald's drinking was also becoming more of a problem. The couple's good friends, Sara and Gerald Murphy, wrote letters to Scott, warning him he would no longer be welcome in their house if he did not clean up his act.[12]

During this time, F. Scott Fitzgerald was hard at work on his next novel. Amazingly, despite all the distractions he faced in his personal life, this novel would prove to be the greatest work of his career—and one of the greatest novels in the history of American literature.

THE
GREAT
AMERICAN
NOVEL

Writers and scholars of American literature often refer to the "Great American Novel." It is supposed to be a novel which somehow catalogues and sums up the archetypal American experience. Many contemporary critics, writers, and readers argue that the American experience is so varied that there is no way that a "Great American Novel" could ever be written. Still, when people make lists of books that would qualify for such a title, one that is always near or at the top of the list is F. Scott Fitzgerald's *The Great Gatsby*.

Despite some real-life parallels, *The Great Gatsby* is actually one of the least autobiographical of Fitzgerald's works. Traces of Fitzgerald's experiences are incorporated, certainly, but it is a marvelous work of imagination—a major creative step for the author.

Fitzgerald himself believed when he was working on it that it would be his greatest achievement. His editor, Maxwell Perkins, was equally excited by the manuscript. Comments from other writers and friends such as Edmund Wilson, H.L. Mencken, and Ernest Hemingway made it clear that *The Great Gatsby* was special. It also caught the favorable attention of the illustrious novelist Edith Wharton. Even writer Gertrude Stein sent Fitzgerald a letter quietly singing his praises—a massive accomplishment, as Stein's negativity was legendary.[1]

The reviews were stellar. Fitzgerald and his publisher had the highest expectations for the book's success. Scott was earning nearly $2,000 for each story he published; no one saw any reason why *Gatsby* would not be a blockbuster and make him even richer. The film rights alone sold for $17,000.

THE GREAT GATSBY

The Great Gatsby opens with a soliloquy of sorts from the book's narrator, Nick Carraway. Nick is a young man who has moved to West Egg—a small, wealthy town on New York's Long Island. It is a commuting town, filled with people who make their money in the city and with the less-well-off locals. Nick lives alone, trying to make a go of it on his own for the first time. Nick graduated from Yale and then fought in World War I. When the war ended, he left his family out West and moved to the East Coast to find work in investment banking. He seems to be a well-grounded, stable young man.

It is seemingly a matter of chance that Nick meets Jay Gatsby, who owns the mansion next door to Nick's rented home. Nick knows nothing about his neighbor except that he throws huge parties. Nick first takes notice of Gatsby early in the novel, before the two actually meet, shortly after visiting his cousin Daisy in East Egg.

soliloquy—*A literary character's speech made as if the person is alone. Often used in dramatic plays as a device to expose a character's private thoughts to the audience.*

NICK AND THE BUCHANANS

Daisy and Tom Buchanan are a handsome couple. Nick adores his cousin Daisy, but has mixed feelings about Tom, whom he knew in college. One afternoon in their house, Nick meets a friend of theirs, Jordan Baker, a woman who is a professional golfer. Learning that Nick lives in West Egg, Baker says that he must know Gatsby. Hearing the name, Daisy seems to snap to attention. Nick admits that Gatsby is his neighbor, but says they have never met.

Nick learns that the Buchanan marriage is complicated. Tom apparently has a mistress. Nick, feeling rather uncomfortable upon learning this, is relieved to leave their house. It is on his way home that he first sees Gatsby, who is standing outside his house, gazing at the lights in East Egg.

Shortly afterward, Nick reluctantly meets Tom Buchanan's mistress, Myrtle. Her husband, George Wilson, owns a gas station. Nick describes, at some length, a merchant's sign near Wilson's gas station, on the road through town to New York. The land, he says, is nothing more than a valley of ashes—with everything gray. Above it all are the eyes of Doctor T. J. Eckleburg, "blue and gigantic—their retinas are one yard high. They look out of no face, but, instead, from a pair of enormous yellow spectacles. . . . over the solemn dumping ground."[2]

Nick Carraway proves an unusual narrator because he seems unbiased despite his personal involvement in the tale's action. The reader is expected to fully trust Carraway's story. As he, himself, proclaims, he is "one of the few honest people that I have ever known."[3]

NICK AND GATSBY

Nick is eventually invited to a party at Gatsby's mansion and he attends, curious about Gatsby, and not wishing to appear rude by refusing. He is surprised by how crowded it is. One of the more amusing sections of the book is Nick's list of people who attended one of Gatsby's parties. The list is quite long and reads like a society gossip column.

After a while, Nick grows embarrassed that he has not met his host. A man at the party strikes up a conversation with Nick, and only after several minutes does the man realize that Nick has no idea who he is. The stranger is Gatsby, who quickly apologizes for being a poor host and not introducing himself sooner. The episode is comic—both innocent and foreboding at the same time.

Shortly afterward, Jordan Baker meets Nick for lunch one day and tells him the story of Gatsby's relationship with Daisy. Gatsby's love for Daisy, she tells him, dates to 1917. Gatsby hopes to win her back and pick up exactly where they left off. Jordan tells Nick about Gatsby's plan: he has asked Jordan to arrange for Nick to bring Daisy to Nick's place. The scheme is for Gatsby to drop by while Daisy is there.

Nick agrees to the plan, which does not run too smoothly at first, but eventually the three of them—Nick, Daisy, and Gatsby—find their way to Gatsby's house. Here Fitzgerald uses some of his growing skills as a writer to show the effect Gatsby has on Daisy:

> He took out a pile of shirts and began throwing them one by one, before us, shirts of sheer linen

and thick silk and fine flannel, which lost their folds as they fell and covered the table in many-colored disarray. . . . Daisy bent her head into the shirts and began to cry stormily.

"They're such beautiful shirts," she sobbed.[4]

THE MYSTERY OF GATSBY

Despite Nick's fondness for him, questions remain about Jay Gatsby. Nick hears many fantastic rumors about Gatsby's past: some say Gatsby was a German spy; others say he is a murderer. Some insist he is a well-educated man who went to Oxford University. Eventually Gatsby confesses to Nick that it is all untrue: he is merely James Gatz of North Dakota. Originally from an undistinguished background out West, he has made himself into a wealthy man, all for the sake of winning Daisy.

Nick muses on Gatsby's evolution, supposing that James Gatz conceived his Gatsby identity at a young age. Nick ominously informs us that Gatsby will remain faithful to this conception "to the end."[5]

DAISY'S CHOICE

The action of the novel begins to build toward a confrontation as Tom, Daisy, Jordan, Nick, and Gatsby all gather at the Buchanan home. It is hot, and the group sits drinking icy gin rickeys. The Buchanans' daughter, Pammy, makes a brief appearance—which seems to unnerve Gatsby—before she is quickly taken away by her nanny. Eventually, the group decides to go for a drive and they load themselves into two cars.

Stopping for gasoline at George Wilson's gas station, Tom has a disconcerting conversation with Wilson, who announces that he and his wife are planning to move out West. He has discovered his wife's infidelity and is determined to take her away with him and start anew. At first Nick assumes that Wilson is accusing Tom of being Myrtle's lover—but then realizes that Wilson has not added it all up yet. Then he notices that Myrtle is watching them all, glaring with "jealous terror" at Jordan Baker, whom she mistakenly assumes is Daisy.[6]

They continue into the city in the two cars, and lounge awkwardly at the Plaza Hotel. There, a showdown finally takes place between Tom and Gatsby. Daisy confesses her love for Gatsby, along with her disdain for her husband, Tom—but this is not enough for Gatsby. He insists that Daisy tell Tom that she never loved him at all, which she cannot do. Tom sees this as a victory. He allows Gatsby to drive Daisy home in his yellow coupe, while he, Jordan, and Nick travel back in his car.

101

GATSBY'S DREAM UNRAVELS

On the way back home, Tom, Nick, and Jordan come upon the aftermath of a horrible accident. Myrtle Wilson has been run over by a yellow coupe. The driver never even stopped. Nick naturally assumes that Gatsby has accidentally killed Myrtle.

Later, as Nick is leaving the Buchanan house, Gatsby appears. He tells Nick that it was Daisy who had been driving the car and accidentally killed Myrtle. He asks Nick to look in on Daisy for him, which he does. Peering through a window, Nick sees Tom and Daisy eating fried chicken together and talking. Nick returns to Gatsby and lets him know that Daisy appears to be alright. Gatsby assures Nick that he, of course, will take the blame for the accident in order to protect Daisy. Even after everything that has transpired, Gatsby still hopes that he and Daisy will somehow be together.

Gatsby's faith, of course, is badly misplaced. The next day, George Wilson goes to the Buchanan house in search of the owner of the yellow coupe that ran down his wife, Myrtle. At this point, Wilson believes that the owner of the car must have also been Myrtle's lover. Tom Buchanan directs Wilson to Gatsby's house. Wilson then sneaks onto Gatsby's property, where he fatally shoots Gatsby and then turns the gun on himself, committing suicide.

A DISILLUSIONED NICK

In the wake of Gatsby's murder, Nick is one of just a few people to show Gatsby proper respect in death. Almost no one else attends the funeral. Tom and Daisy have gone and left no forwarding address. The throngs of people who once attended Gatsby's many parties are nowhere to be found. Nick, disgusted with everyone, considers moving back out West.

Some time later, Nick runs into Tom Buchanan in New York. Nick can now clearly see that Tom and Daisy are cruel and careless people who worry about no one but themselves and no longer hides his disapproval of them.

As the novel ends and Nick is about to leave New York, he stops and considers the coastline. He wonders what the Dutch explorers thought when they first saw the New World. He thinks about the dreams that they must have had and seems to express cynicism over whether or not any dream can ever truly be realized. In this way, Fitzgerald makes the broader symbolism of the novel most clear: that the American Dream is, in reality, unattainable.

Themes of *The Great Gatsby*

In *The Great Gatsby* Fitzgerald repeats and builds on themes from earlier works. The novel's end, when Nick Carraway recalls America as "The New World," recalls similar imagery in "May Day." Nick also observes that although the story he tells seems to be a tale of the East Coast, it is really about people from the Midwest who come back East to pursue their dreams. The idea that you can re-create yourself as a totally new person—as Gatsby tried to do—without any sense of history betrays a Western sensibility. Out West, everything is so new that nothing has any history. Back East, however, one apparently cannot escape the past.

The significance of financial wealth in the novel also warrants examination, as it is once again a most prevalent theme. One critic notes that the message behind this theme in Fitzgerald's works concerns more than mere materialism. The Buchanans serve as an excellent illustration of this. Though they are obviously very wealthy, the Buchanans are not materialistic in the sense in that they do not boast about their many possessions or flaunt their wealth overly much in the novel. Rather, money is simply a tool that allows them to live their lives as they please—it is the "justification of their consuming snobberies."[7] Those from poor or working class backgrounds (like Gatsby and Myrtle Wilson) will often make the mistake of viewing money as the "alchemical reagent that transmutes the ordinary worthlessness of life."[8] In other words, Fitzgerald is once again demonstrating in *Gatsby* that financial wealth does not guarantee moral virtue. If anything, he seems to suggest that there is an inverse relationship between the two qualities. The less-than-wealthy characters of his fiction almost invariably possess more virtue than the wealthy ones. However, such characters rarely seem to recognize this fact for themselves.

SYMBOLISM IN *THE GREAT GATSBY*

The novel's use of color as symbol is similar to its use in *The Beautiful and Damned*. At various times, the colors work to convey multiple meanings, to stand for character traits, or to enrich atmosphere. Daisy's white wardrobe, the image of the green light across the bay, the yellow coupe—each color represents a character trait or idea. The Valley of Ashes over which the oculist's sign hovers is ashen, or gray, evoking death and desperation. Daisy's white clothes symbolize a surface purity of the ideal she represents to Gatsby (through Daisy's later behavior, the reader may come to view Daisy's "whiteness" as ironic). The green light Gatsby watches obsessively evokes the ideas of dreams and hope; the green symbolizes the innocence they once had, and, the characters learn, have irretrievably lost. Yellow—as in Gatsby's yellow coupe, and Dr. Eckleburg's yellow eyeglass frames—symbolizes cowardliness and deceit. The rich rainbow of shirt colors that explode from Gatsby's armoire emphasize the richness and beauty of Gatsby's feelings for Daisy.

No other symbol in the novel, however, works as clearly and powerfully as the eyes of Dr. Eckleburg watching over West Egg. After Myrtle Wilson's death, her husband, George, recalls for his friend, Michaelis, a conversation they had recently shared:

> "I said, 'God knows what you've been doing, everything you've been doing. You may fool me, but you can't fool God!'"
>
> Standing beside him, Michaelis saw with a shock that he was looking at the eyes of Doctor T. J. Eckleburg, which had just emerged, pale and enormous, from the dissolving night.
>
> "God sees everything," repeated Wilson.[9]

NARRATIVE STYLE OF GATSBY

Fitzgerald's decision to write *The Great Gatsby* in the first person is interesting because it adds a much stronger sense of emotional involvement for the reader. Nick's position as the narrator of *The Great Gatsby* also means that the reader has no choice but to hear Gatsby's story from Nick's perspective.

With a seemingly omniscient, third-person narrator, the reader would have to accept the narrator's words as fact. But with a first-person narrator who is involved in the action, readers are more challenged to make their own judgements of the characters and their actions.

Though Nick claims he is honest by nature, the reader sees him enabling many acts of dishonesty and deception—he goes out with Tom and his mistress, Myrtle; helps arrange a clandestine meeting between Gatsby and his married cousin, Daisy; and enjoys a romantic relationship with Jordan Baker, whom he, himself, acknowledges is a casual liar and a golf cheat.

When Nick is finally moved to voice a strong value judgment, however, the effect is made that much stronger as a result. Near the novel's end, when he proclaims that Gatsby is worth all the others put together, the reader is inclined to agree, having experienced the events of the novel through Nick's eyes and been propelled along with him toward the same conclusion.

Use of Language

Perhaps more than any other of Fitzgerald's works, language plays a large role in *The Great Gatsby*. The way the characters speak, their accents and choice of words, are often revealing.

Normally, one would associate well-mannered speech with the wealthier, upper class and, conversely, use of slang and swearing with the lower classes. In an ironic twist, Fitzgerald reverses these trends in *Gatsby*. Born and raised in the Midwestern United States and from a working-class background, Gatsby always speaks in a polite and mannered language, often with a British affect. His use of the word "old sport" and even the occasional "chap" are good illustrations of this. Tom Buchanan, despite his wealthy and privileged upbringing, usually speaks using rough language and tone. (Note, for example, the unashamed ease with which he uses the word "bitch" in chapter two.)

The significance of language is less obvious with other characters. Besides Gatsby and Tom Buchanan, Daisy's use of language is probably the most notable. Her speech often carries a dreamlike, almost ethereal quality—drifting, flighty, careless, and carefree. From early in the novel, when she expresses a desire to plan something but has no clear idea of what that something is, to near the novel's end when she describes her daughter as a "dream," the idea is reinforced throughout the story.

FITZGERALD'S VIEW OF GATSBY

Fitzgerald felt that *The Great Gatsby* was a flawed masterpiece and, at different points in his life, discussed the problems he saw in the book. Among them were things such as the fact that there is almost no description of the characters' physical appearances (the reader does not know the color of Gatsby's hair, for example, or Nick's height). This is because Fitzgerald wrote the book with this motto in mind: "Action Is Character."[10] As a result, the reader is meant to "see" the characters less for their superficial features and more for their inner character, as demonstrated by their behavior. Fitzgerald later questioned whether this technique was effective.

Ultimately, the novel was published to considerable praise and Fitzgerald was never more proud of anything he had done. His story of modern New York was completely original. Novels of New York manners published in the previous thirty years were mostly of the sort written by Edith Wharton: very precise studies on the social mores of the upper class. The rest of the population did not exist for these writers. Fitzgerald was the first to acknowledge the sweep and range of backgrounds of the people in New York and its environs. He observed, fairly and accurately, details of speech, attire, and attitude which were never previously captured in a novel.[11] In this respect, *The Great Gatsby* is as much a work of social history as it is a work of fiction. Because of his own entry, from a Midwestern background, into New York society as it was evolving, Fitzgerald was perhaps uniquely equipped to write a book like *The Great Gatsby*.[12] It is both an accomplished work of fiction and a great work of social relevance.

The novel also represented an improvement stylistically. *The Great Gatsby* is a smoother book than Fitzgerald's previous novels; lacking some of the jumpiness—in terms of plot, structure, and timing—of earlier works. Critic Kenneth Eble described the novel's structure as having a "tight inevitability."[13] The first-person narration probably helped a great deal in this regard, and one can only speculate as to why Fitzgerald did not write in the first-person more often.

THE POETRY OF *GATSBY*

Some of the passages in *Gatsby* capture some of Fitzgerald's most beautiful and romantic prose. This passage, which describes when Gatsby first fell in love with Daisy, may very well be Fitzgerald at his most poetic:

> His heart beat faster and faster as Daisy's white face came up to his own. He knew that when he kissed this girl, and forever wed his unutterable visions to her perishable breath, his mind would never romp again like the mind of God. So he waited, listening for a moment longer to the tuning fork that had been struck upon a star. Then he kissed her. At his lips' touch she blossomed for him like a flower and the incarnation was complete.[14]

Other passages in the novel are written in a similarly masterful fashion. Return, for example, to the scene discussed earlier, where Gatsby is emptying his wardrobe for Daisy, Fitzgerald could have written simply: "He took all of his shirts and threw them on the table." Clearly, however, the emotional effect is lost. Even minor editing of the line would rob it of much of its power: "He threw the shirts, one by one, until they covered the table in a many-colored disarray of sheer linen, thick silk, and flannel." Although it is more descriptive, this line is still not as strong as the original. Fitzgerald's final version has the peaks and rolls necessary to sweep the reader along, ending with the tantalizing alliteration: "fine flannel, which lost their folds as they fell."

alliteration—*The repetition of sounds in two or more neighboring words.*

111

There is no question that Fitzgerald's ear for language and sentence structure had reached a new level with *The Great Gatsby*. A writer who produced only one work of this caliber could rest assured that his literary star would never fade.

THE EXPATRIATES

After finishing *Gatsby*, the Fitzgeralds relocated to Paris. In the mid-1920s, Paris was filled with American expatriates—Americans who, for economic or social reasons, were living in inexpensive and permissive Europe. There was a large community of writers and artists there, and they were joined by the Fitzgeralds, with little daughter Scottie in tow.

During these days, a legendary friendship began when Ernest Hemingway, another young writer, met Scott Fitzgerald. The two men knew and admired each other's work, and found they had many common interests. They enjoyed each other's company. Where Fitzgerald was delicate, sensitive, and clever, Hemingway was often blunt and harsh. Still, the two men got along well. Fitzgerald was very impressed with Hemingway's work, and helped get his first short story collection published in New York. In turn, Hemingway introduced Fitzgerald to Gertrude Stein, a famous American expatriate writer. She lived with her partner, Alice B. Toklas. They were known for their parties and intelligent conversation. Anyone who mattered came to see them. Stein wrote extremely experimental books. She acted as a kind of mentor who took many young authors under her wing.

Scott and Zelda Fitzgerald tried to enjoy their time in Paris. While their marriage was still strained from Zelda's affair, the anticipated success of *The Great Gatsby* offered the family bright hopes for the future. Incredibly, however, *The Great Gatsby* proved a disaster with the public. Fitzgerald was bitterly disappointed by this. His publisher in Great Britain would not even issue the novel, saying that as good as Fitzgerald was, he did not make the publisher any money.

Scott and Zelda grew desperate. By 1926, they were moving every few months, hoping that the next place would bring happiness and luck.

LOST AND WANDERING

Scott and Zelda Fitzgerald were social butterflies, with friends all over America and Europe. Scott and Zelda were trying to create new lives, always in new locales, but also trying to recapture their happier days in the past.

A LOST GENERATION

Gertrude Stein described the Fitzgeralds, and their friend Hemingway, as being members of a "lost generation." The phrase was used to categorize those modern writers searching for meaning in the pervasive disillusionment that existed in the aftermath of World War I. Like so many others of their generation, these writers were struggling to come to terms with a postwar world which had changed faster and more dramatically than anything their elders had ever experienced.

Stein was one of the leaders of this artistic movement; Gerald and Sara Murphy, who mostly lived on the French Riviera, were also pillars of the community. The Murphys were kind, sophisticated, and a very devoted couple. The Fitzgeralds spent a great deal of time with the Murphys, despite the fact they were constantly moving all over France and Italy, trying to live as cheaply as possible in the wake of the rather surprising commercial failure of *The Great Gatsby*.

"THE RICH ARE DIFFERENT FROM YOU AND ME"

The Fitzgeralds had several major problems, all of which seemed to aggravate one another. First, the couple never had enough money. One reason for this was that Fitzgerald's work habits were erratic. One of the chief causes of this was Fitzgerald's drinking, which was out of control. (At this time, alcoholism was not regarded as a disease, as it is today. If alcoholism affected one's livelihood, it was regarded more as a personal, moral failure.) The Fitzgeralds would continue to argue about money, which made Scott drink still more. Then, when he could not work, money would get tighter. It was a vicious circle.[1]

Fitzgerald's financial struggles only seemed to strengthen his ideas about the importance of money. As we have seen, Fitzgerald viewed personal wealth

F. Scott and Zelda with their daughter, Scottie, in Paris in the 1920s.

almost as a gift from God and—at various times in his fiction—portrayed this "gift" as an indication of both divine favor and a divine curse. Fitzgerald's treatment of the themes of wealth and social class are unique, as illustrated in the now-famous conversation he once had with Ernest Hemingway, when he noted: "The rich are different from you and me." Hemingway's simple response to this was: "Yes, they have more money."[2]

Although Fitzgerald and Hemingway both wrote about the virtues (or their lack) in modern man, Hemingway never saw any connection between virtue and wealth. Fitzgerald, on the other hand, could almost never separate the two.

"THE RICH BOY"

Fitzgerald's conversation with Hemingway probably served as the inspiration for the opening of Fitzgerald's story "The Rich Boy," published in early 1926 in *Red Book* magazine and, soon after, in the 1926 story collection, *All the Sad Young Men*. It begins:

> Let me tell you about the very rich. They are different from you and me. They possess and enjoy early, and it does something to them, makes them soft where we are hard, and cynical where we are trustful, in a way that, unless you were born rich, it is very difficult to understand. They think, deep

in their hearts, that they are better than we are because we had to discover the compensations and refuges of life for ourselves. Even when they enter deep into our world or sink below us, the still think that they are better than we are. They are different.[3]

The protagonist of "The Rich Boy" is a young man named Anson Hunter. The narrator of the tale is Hunter's classmate, and he tells Hunter's story sympathetically. Hunter, with his New York family's money and connections, goes to Yale and then works on Wall Street. He becomes attached to a young woman named Paula, who seems perfect for him. But Anson's drinking becomes uncontrollable, and Paula will not stand for it. She refuses to marry him, quickly marrying a solid Boston man instead.

Anson, heartbroken, dates other women, but does not fall in love. His next girlfriend also leaves him to marry another man. Years go by, and Anson spends most of his time drunkenly trying to recapture his youthful heyday. Like Gatsby in his attempt to recover his youth, Anson becomes pathetic. Everyone Anson knows has grown up, faced their fates and responsibilities. His friends who make mistakes admit them, and move on to better lives for the experience. Paula's first marriage ends disastrously, but when Anson runs into her by chance one afternoon, she is blissfully remarried and pregnant. He cannot believe it, and when Paula says she had never been in love until she met her new husband, it hurts Anson.

Anson's mother's death takes a financial toll on the Hunters: taxes and the division of the estate between Anson and his siblings mean that there is no more family fortune. Suddenly, they are no longer wealthy.

When Paula dies in childbirth, Anson realizes he will never marry. His only love was irreplaceable. He dates girls who are too young for him. The narrator concludes by wondering how and why Anson gets involved with these young women. One would imagine they'd want more than some wreck of a thirty-year old, which is just what Anson is, though he does not realize it: "Perhaps they promised that there would always be women in the world who would spend their brightest, freshest, rarest hours to nurse and protect that superiority he cherished in his heart."[4]

THEMES OF "THE RICH BOY"

"The Rich Boy" is poignant. Clearly, Fitzgerald's personal circumstances had weathered and aged him and he used characters like Anson Hunter to capture his own experience. The story features many of the universal themes that typified Fitzgerald's fiction at this point: primarily wealth and its connection to the loss of youth and beauty. Anson's lost promise also parallels the lost promise F. Scott Fitzgerald was feeling in his own life.

Fitzgerald's *All the Sad Young Men* contained some of his finest writing, including "The Rich Boy," "Winter Dreams," and "Absolution" (one of Fitzgerald's most religious works), and the collection was well-reviewed. It sold respectably and earned the Fitzgeralds a much-needed $4,000.

The Fitzgeralds were back living in the U.S. in January 1927 when a tempting business offer came Fitzgerald's way. At this time, famous writers had been earning huge sums of money writing screenplays in Hollywood, with work that was said to be quick and easy. So when Fitzgerald received an offer from United Artists, he and Zelda were thrilled. The studio offered him an advance of $3,500 and another $12,500 if his work was accepted—a staggering offer at the time. The family quickly boarded a train, bound for California.

LIFE IN HOLLYWOOD

Hollywood was full of temptation. Fitzgerald engaged in the drunken behavior that had caused trouble in Europe. On one occasion, Fitzgerald prepared a meal for friends by cooking several watches and some jewelry in tomato soup.[5] Fitzgerald's drunkenness lost him friends and valuable Hollywood connections. Meanwhile, Zelda's emotional state continued to deteriorate.

Zelda had always tended to be flighty and careless, but in 1927, her actions began to have dangerous consequences when she burned some of her clothes in a bathtub. Part of the reason for Zelda's erratic behavior were her suspicions that Scott was being unfaithful. The truth was that Zelda was losing her grip on reality.

United Artists wound up passing on the movie Fitzgerald wrote, *Lipstick*, and the Fitzgeralds did not get the $12,500. There was no reason for them to stay in Hollywood any longer, but they were afraid to go to New York or Europe. So the Fitzgeralds wound up moving to Delaware, where they were within reasonable traveling distance of relatives (Zelda's family was still in Montgomery, and Scott's parents were then living in Washington, D.C.).

A NEW NOVEL

At this time, Fitzgerald was working on a new novel, and friends who read parts of the manuscript thought it showed promise. The work went slowly. After a year in Delaware, the Fitzgeralds decided to go back to Europe. They went to Paris in April 1928, but stayed only a few months and returned briefly to Delaware. When the lease on the Delaware house ended in 1929, the Fitzgeralds went back to Europe. They sailed to Italy and moved from there to France, where they spent several months.

The year 1929 was the beginning of the end for the Fitzgeralds. They were drinking and fighting so much that they alarmed friends. Zelda's mental and physical strength had been exhausted after years of hard living. Scott Fitzgerald's professional prospects were also deteriorating. While *The Saturday Evening Post* was paying Fitzgerald $4,000 per story in 1929, his short stories were taking time away from working on his novel, which he knew was more important.

In April 1930 Zelda had a nervous breakdown. Scott brought Zelda to the finest psychiatric hospital in Switzerland, which cost him $1,000 per month. Fitzgerald churned out stories, and sold them for large sums to support Zelda.

Zelda was discharged from a Swiss hospital in September 1931. She was diagnosed as a schizophrenic but her doctors said it was safe for her to rejoin her husband. The couple then relocated to Montgomery, Alabama, to be near Zelda's family. Fitzgerald did not want to live near Zelda's family—they did not approve of him—but he put his personal differences with them aside in the hopes that they might help Zelda.

Shortly after the move, in the fall of 1931, a

Hollywood producer offered Fitzgerald another job. Excited by the opportunity, Fitzgerald went to California. Unable to control his drinking, however, Fitzgerald was fired after five weeks and he was back in Alabama by Christmastime.

For a few months, the Fitzgeralds were on good terms. Scott's short stories earned good money, and Zelda seemed stable and happy. Although the death of Zelda's father in November 1931 was difficult for her, Scott observed, in a letter to one of her European doctors, that the time from summer 1931 to early 1932 was the happiest time they had ever shared together.[6]

THE END OF HAPPINESS

Sadly, in early 1932, Zelda began to experience hallucinations. In February, she checked into the psychiatric institute at Johns Hopkins University, in Baltimore, Maryland. After she was discharged a few months later, Fitzgerald rented a comfortable house for them in a Baltimore suburb. Then, in the summer of 1933, Zelda accidentally set fire to the house—an ominous sign of things to come.

Fitzgerald's work on a new novel, however, was going well. Since the house was still habitable, they stayed there until the novel was completed. Then they moved to Baltimore. In 1933, Zelda's brother committed suicide, which affected Zelda badly. She was institutionalized again in February 1934. Dissatisfied with her treatment, Fitzgerald transferred her to another clinic, up the Hudson River from New York City, where her condition seemed to improve.

During this time, while Zelda was in and out of hospitals, Fitzgerald was trying to solve his own professional problems. He also sought medical help for his alcoholism.

CHAPTER 9

THE DARKEST NIGHT

ender Is the Night was published on April 12, 1934. Nine years in the works, it was different from Fitzgerald's previous novels. Like *The Beautiful and Damned*, it was highly autobiographical, but it was denser than his previous work. Its characters were multidimensional, and the relationships were more complex. As Fitzgerald's life had grown more complicated and confusing, so did the lives of his characters. Moreover, his writing skills had improved significantly.

TENDER IS THE NIGHT

Tender Is the Night focuses on the relationship of a married couple, Dick and Nicole Diver. They live the high life in France. Early in the novel, they meet a teenage actress, Rosemary Hoyt. Sophisticated beyond her years, Rosemary becomes emotionally involved in the Divers' marriage and, eventually, falls in love with Dick.

Over the course of the novel, Fitzgerald jumps from one phase of the Divers' relationship to another, starting the tale after the Divers have been married awhile. While they have children of their own, the couple also acts as "parents" to a circle of troubled expatriate friends (a role Fitzgerald saw being filled in real life by Gerald and Sara Murphy—who served as inspirations, in part, for the Divers). These friends include characters such as Abe North, an alcoholic songwriter; novelist Albert McKisco and his wife, Violet; Tommy Barban, a mercenary in the war; and Nicole's sister, Baby Warren, whose main interest in life is money. All of the Divers' friends have character flaws which Fitzgerald uses to convey corruption. In each case, the characters act badly, but seem to find themselves amused by their own terrible behavior when they should, in fact, be alarmed and ashamed of themselves.

mercenary—*A soldier who fights for money; or, more generally, a person who works for the highest bidder with no other motivation than greed.*

In the novel's second section, the reader learns that Dick and Nicole met when Nicole was in a mental institution and Dick was her doctor. Nicole's emotional problems were caused by her father, who forced her into an incestuous relationship. As Nicole's doctor, Dick should not become emotionally involved with her, but he does. While he realizes that having a romantic relationship with a patient is unethical, he cannot stop himself—Nicole is irresistible to him. And just as Fitzgerald's real-life marriage to Zelda seemed, for a time, to be beneficial to Zelda's mental state, so too does Nicole's marriage to Dick calm her for a while. Eventually, however, Dick's affair with Rosemary unhinges Nicole.

In the final section of the novel, the Divers, along with their friends, slide into worse trouble. The expatriates have run-ins with Italian police and are involved in murders, serious brawls, and other smaller but unsavory episodes. Through it all, Dick tries to reconnect himself with his medical practice and go back to his old, moral lifestyle, but is distracted by the various difficulties of his friends and family.

Ultimately, Dick winds up completely losing sight of his values, his sense of self, and his family. The book concludes with Nicole leaving Dick to marry Tommy Barban and Dick returning to America and going into private practice. He refuses to take any of Nicole's money and deliberately loses touch with her. He works as a doctor in a series of small towns in upstate New York and slowly, as the years pass, he fades away into obscurity.

FITZGERALD'S DEVELOPMENT

Tender Is the Night is Fitzgerald's most mature and complex work yet. The novel does not rely on stylistic gimmickry, as *This Side of Paradise* did. The story itself is complicated and the writing captures its themes gracefully and boldly. The conversations that Dr. Diver and his colleagues have about various patients are sophisticated and blunt. Rosemary's actions, which are the flapper's antics gone to extremes, are also candidly described. *Tender Is the Night* is a difficult work, with its images of corruption, incest, and sin. It contains almost none of the romantic imagery present in his previous novel, *The Great Gatsby*.

PARALLELS BETWEEN THE DIVERS AND FITZGERALDS

Despite the fact they were partially modeled after the Murphys, the Divers have much more in common with Scott and Zelda Fitzgerald. The fact that Dick is a psychiatrist is telling: through Dick Diver, Fitzgerald can be seen as psychoanalyzing his own life and marriage.

The Divers' marital difficulties mirror those of the

Fitzgeralds' most closely in Nicole's mental and emotional instability. As Ernest Hemingway would later write: "If [Fitzgerald] could write a book as fine as *The Great Gatsby* I was sure he could write an even better one. I did not know Zelda yet, and so I did not know the terrible odds that were against him. But we were to find them out soon enough."[1]

THEMES OF *TENDER IS THE NIGHT*

Fitzgerald derived the novel's title from a line from John Keats' poem, "Ode to a Nightingale." Keats was one of the major poets of the Romantic period, whose poems often dealt with the resolution of eternal longings in a fleeting, transitory world. In "Ode to a Nightingale," he described how the sound of a singing bird transforms him by conjuring thoughts of his own mortality.

Much like the poem, many of the characters in *Tender Is the Night* are similarly haunted by the specter of death. Fitzgerald even makes use of the nightingale/bird symbol to illustrate this. Abe North mentions that McKisco was "plagued by the nightingale" when he agreed to duel Tommy Barban, for example. Also, when Rosemary goes shopping with Nicole, the lovebird on Nicole's shoulder seems to compel her to recount her sister's near-fatal attack of appendicitis.

The novel's title is also made all the more appropriate by Fitzgerald's use of night and darkness as literary devices throughout the narrative. Generally speaking, the characters are living in darkness in as much as they are "blind"—unable to see the terrible consequences their actions will have. The night also comes to symbolize the hidden forces at work beneath the surface action.

The Symbolic Moon

The moon is often a symbol in the story as well, one closely tied to the aforementioned night symbolism. While night represents the hidden and mysterious, the moon, more specifically, seems to represent erotic passion and love.

When Nicole shares a romantic rendezvous with Dick at the sanitarium, she is described as stepping out of the woods and into the "clear moonlight." Later, at the moment Rosemary first falls in love with Dick, she is "suspended in the moonshine" of a "limpid, black night." Then, when Nicole begins her affair with Tommy Barban, the two are described as being "tangled with love in the moonlight."

SEXUAL METAPHORS

The incest theme is a recurring one throughout *Tender Is the Night*. At times it is overt, as with Nicole's relationship with her father, Devereux Warren. At other times, it is more subliminal, as with Dick's relationships with Nicole and, later, Rosemary, who plays a childlike part to Dick's more paternal role. (Even Rosemary's movie, *Daddy's Girl*, hints at the incest theme.)

When they first meet, Dick is supposed to fill the role of healer with Nicole and help her get past the difficulties she faces in the wake of the abuse she suffered at her father's hands. By becoming romantically involved with Nicole while she is his patient, Dick effectively commits another kind of incest—this is where Dick's corruption begins. When he becomes involved with Rosemary later on, he is repeating the earlier pattern with Nicole—and, in so doing, repeating the same error.

WAR METAPHORS

Dick Diver has roots to what was, at that time, the three major wars of American history: the Revolution, the Civil War, and World War I. Diver is descended from Revolutionary War hero Anthony Wayne; is compared (albeit unfavorably) to Union

Civil War General Ulysses S. Grant; and at one point describes his state upon waking from a bad dream as shell shock, akin to that suffered by the soldiers of World War I.

These war references are metaphors, intended to represent the physical and moral erosion of the Western world. World War I references in particular allude to such erosion, as it was the most devastating war in history up to that point and left the Western world terribly weakened and disillusioned. In this way, Dick Diver, himself, might be viewed as symbolizing the modern, Western world—disillusioned, corrupt, and slowly wasting away.

Public Reaction to *Tender is the Night*

Tender Is the Night sold respectably, but it did not sell well enough to earn back the large sum of money that Fitzgerald owed Scribner's, his publisher. One contributing factor to the novel's relatively low sales may have been that it was published as America was suffering through the Great Depression. People who were facing poverty and starvation were probably not very interested in reading about the difficulties faced by wealthy Americans living in Europe. Matthew Bruccoli notes in his biography of Fitzgerald that a "mood of loss and waste pervades" *Tender Is the Night.*[2] This dark mood also undoubtedly hurt sales. Since expectations for the book were high, its low sales were very disappointing to Fitzgerald and Scribner's.

FITZGERALD'S TROUBLES

Fitzgerald, troubled by his lagging career, was also worried about his own health. Feeling sick and suspecting he had tuberculosis, he spent a month at a health resort in North Carolina.

For all the frustration Fitzgerald felt about the sales of his novels, his stories still sold for considerable sums of money. In fact, financially speaking, 1931 had been a remarkable year for Fitzgerald: his accounting for that year shows he earned more than $37,000.[3] This is all the more impressive considering the country was in the middle of a massive economic depression.

In March 1935, a new collection of Fitzgerald's

The Great Depression was a period of terrible poverty that began with the stock market crash in October 1929 and persisted throughout the 1930s. The Great Depression finally ended as World War II began in late 1939. The increased production of war materials during this time provided many jobs and put large amounts of money back into circulation.

stories, *Taps At Reveille*, was published. Though the stories had sold individually for a great deal of money, the collection did not sell well, going through only one printing. Considering the table of contents, this seems incredible now. Included in this collection were the stories "Babylon Revisited," "Crazy Sunday," and "The Last of the Belles," along with a number of stories about two recurring characters, Basil and Josephine. Today, "Babylon Revisited" and "Crazy Sundays" are among Fitzgerald's most anthologized stories. That they were so ignored by the reading public in 1935 is remarkable.

By this time, Scott Fitzgerald's standard of living was very low, as a result of having to pay for Zelda's hospitalization. He lived on canned meat and drank heavily. He spent most of the mid-1930s moving frequently around the Mid-Atlantic region, writing stories for money, desperate to pay bills. In 1936 his mother died, which, despite their complex relationship, was a blow for Fitzgerald. Life began to seem even grimmer.

Living in cheap apartments or low-rent hotels, Fitzgerald began to work on some essays. He wrote about life, genius and its uses, and money. Some pieces were comical; all of them were intelligent and well-written. The essays were published in *Esquire* by a sympathetic editor, Arnold Gingrich, who hoped that these mature essays would bode well for Fitzgerald's future.[4] Articles such as "Show Mr. and Mrs. F. to Number ___" and "Auction—Model 1934" showed a new self-awareness on Fitzgerald's part, which, combined with his mature writing skills, held great artistic potential.

LIFE AND LEGACY

The summer of 1937 brought Fitzgerald an offer from MGM for $1,000 a week to work as a screen-writer. Being $40,000 in debt and needing a steady income, Fitzgerald quickly accepted the offer. He went to Hollywood and stayed a surprisingly long time: a year and a half. He worked on six scripts and earned $88,500. He paid off his debts and started saving money. The savings would see him through the period he planned to work on his next novel.

SHEILAH GRAHAM

In Hollywood, Fitzgerald lived in a hotel on Sunset Boulevard called the Garden of Allah. The hotel was once the residence of many famous people. Famous writers such as Dorothy Parker, Robert Benchley, Nathaniel West, and Aldous Huxley lived there when they wrote screenplays. Actors Greta Garbo, Katharine Hepburn, Humphrey Bogart, and Lauren Bacall also spent time there. It was in 1937 at the

Garden of Allah that Fitzgerald met a woman who became very important to him. Though he had had a number of affairs over the years, few were as significant as his relationship with British journalist Sheilah Graham.

Graham would become Fitzgerald's companion for the rest of his life. She would help Fitzgerald quit drinking and develop better work habits. Though the relationship was difficult at times, it was a great comfort to Fitzgerald.

While earning his living writing for MGM, Fitzgerald also continued to work on his own fiction. These stories did not pay much (most of them sold for a mere $250 each[1]) and they barely kept his name circulating. He had become so obscure people assumed he was dead. Even as a screenwriter, he achieved little notoriety. Only one movie, *Three Comrades*, earned him a screen credit.

The stories Scott worked on in the late 1930s focused primarily on one character: Pat Hobby. Hobby is, in small part, a fictionalized Fitzgerald: a has-been, alcoholic hack writer working in Hollywood. Unlike Fitzgerald, who was ashamed of his bad behavior, Hobby is a greedy loser. Fitzgerald was trying to turn over a new leaf, professionally and personally. Fitzgerald was so consumed with trying

F. Scott Fitzgerald with Sheilah Graham in California.

to shed his earlier persona that he actually considered publishing under a pseudonym (an assumed name).[2]

FINAL YEARS

In 1939 and 1940 Fitzgerald's health was poor. Years of alcoholism had already taken a toll on him, and doctors had diagnosed him with tuberculosis. Then, in November 1940, he had a heart attack. This was followed a month later by a second heart attack. Finally, he suffered a third, fatal attack on December 21, 1940, while he was at home with Sheilah Graham. Fitzgerald had died at the relatively young age of forty-four.

Zelda was in mental institutions for most of Fitzgerald's time in California. She was distraught when he died, and composed letters to his agent and publisher praising her husband and his work. Scottie, aged nineteen, went to the sparsely attended funeral. The world was not mourning F. Scott Fitzgerald. His death was a matter of interest to few people; the newspaper obituaries were brief.

Zelda Fitzgerald died a few years after Scott, in March 1948. A kitchen fire at her hospital spread, and the building burned down. Zelda lost her life in the fire.

HIS LAST NOVEL

At the time Scott Fitzgerald died he was, ironically, just starting to come out of his professional slump. He was working on a novel which he felt good about, titled *The Last Tycoon*. He was writing and publishing stories. He had spent years unhappy, uncomfortable, and obscure after massive fame. It was tragic that, just as things were looking up, he died.

The Last Tycoon was published about a year after Fitzgerald died. It was unfinished but substantial enough to publish. Many critics speculate that, had Fitzgerald lived to complete the work, it could have been his finest novel. *The Last Tycoon* is among the first—and finest— of its genre, the Hollywood novel. Following the story and career of film producer Monroe Stahr, it is the first major work of fiction to deal with Hollywood and the themes that come naturally to that setting.

THE FITZGERALD REVIVAL

When Fitzgerald died, the public was underwhelmed; many had assumed he had died years earlier. Soon after Fitzgerald's demise, however, fellow authors and literary critics began to pay tribute to Fitzgerald's work. Writers Glenway Wescott and John Dos Passos wrote elegant essays in tribute to

Fitzgerald, which were collected with Fitzgerald's essays in *The Crack Up*. American literary critics spoke unanimously of the brilliance of Fitzgerald's novels and stories. The 1940s saw the reprinting of Fitzgerald's novels, which had been unavailable for years (even *The Great Gatsby* had been out of print). By 1949, a full-fledged Fitzgerald revival began in earnest with the publication of Arthur Mizener's biography, *The Far Side of Paradise*.

By the 1950s, F. Scott Fitzgerald's reputation had turned around. No longer viewed as a trivial chronicler of fashion and frippery, he was called an astute observer of American culture and society. Stories by Fitzgerald began to be taught in schools and colleges. Budd Schulberg, who as a young man had worked under Fitzgerald in Hollywood, published *The Disenchanted*, a fictionalized account of Fitzgerald's last days. While not a cheerful book, it nonetheless kept the man and his work in the mind of the reading public.

As the stars of many Lost Generation writers began to fade, Fitzgerald's seemed to burn brighter. The 1960s brought the publication of a number of other memoirs of Paris in the 1920s. (Hemingway's *A Moveable Feast* also featured tales of the Fitzgeralds, although its descriptions of them were not at all flattering—and at times bordered on venomous.)

No matter what people's personal memories of

Fitzgerald may have been, it was universally agreed that his fiction was a remarkable achievement. This position has not changed in the last forty years. Today, F. Scott Fitzgerald is recognized as one of the greatest authors in the history of American literature.

CHRONOLOGY

1896—*September 24*: Francis Scott Key Fitzgerald is born in St. Paul, Minnesota.

1898—Family moves to Buffalo, New York.

1901—Family moves to Syracuse, New York.

1903—Family moves back to Buffalo.

1908—Family returns to St. Paul; F. Scott enrolls at St. Paul Academy in September.

1911—Enters Newman School in Hackensack, New Jersey.

1912—Meets Father Fay.

1913—Enters Princeton University with Class of 1917.

1914—*August*: World War I begins in Europe.
December 25: Meets Ginevra King in St. Paul.

1915—Drops out of Princeton halfway through junior year.

1916—*September*: Returns to Princeton.

1917—*November*: Joins the army as the United States enters World War I; reports to Fort Leavenworth, Kansas; begins novel *The Romantic Egotist*.

1918—*March*: Completes first draft of *The Romantic Egotist* while on leave at Princeton.
April: Transferred to Camp Gordon, Georgia.

June: Reports to Camp Sheridan near Montgomery, Alabama.

July: Meets Zelda Sayre at a country club dance in Montgomery.

November: World War I ends as Germany accepts an armistice on November 11.

1919—*February*: Discharged from the army; moves to New York to work for an advertising agency; informally engaged to Zelda.

April: Visits Zelda in Montgomery; Zelda is reluctant to marry.

June: Zelda breaks engagement.

July: Quits advertising job and returns to St. Paul; rewrites novel.

September: Scribner's accepts *This Side of Paradise*.

1920—Eighteenth Amendment goes into effect; Prohibition begins.

January: Visits Zelda in Montgomery; resumes engagement to Zelda; short stories published in *The Saturday Evening Post*.

March: *This Side of Paradise* is published.

April: Marries Zelda in rectory of St. Patrick's Cathedral in New York.

September: Short-story collection *Flappers and Philosophers* is published.

1921—Daughter, Scottie, is born October 26.

1922—*March*: *The Beautiful and Damned* is published.

September: Second collection of short stories, *Tales of the Jazz Age*, is published.

1923—*November*: Play, *The Vegetable*, fails at tryout in Atlantic City, New Jersey.

1924—Leaves U.S. for Europe with Zelda and Scottie.
Writes first draft of *The Great Gatsby*.
Zelda has affair with French aviator Edouard Jozan.
Revises *The Great Gatsby*.

1925—*April*: *The Great Gatsby* is published.
May: Meets Ernest Hemingway.

1926—Returns with his family to the U.S.

1927—*January*: Moves to Hollywood.

1929—*March*: Returns to Europe.
April: Zelda has first breakdown in Paris, enters clinic.
June: Zelda enters Prangins clinic at Nyon, Switzerland.
October: Stock market crashes; Great Depression begins.

1931—*January*: Death of father, Edward Fitzgerald; returns to the U.S. to attend funeral.
September: Zelda released from Prangins; family returns to U.S.
November: Death of Zelda's father, Anthony Sayre.

1932—*February*: Zelda suffers second breakdown; enters psychiatric clinic in Baltimore.
March: Zelda completes first draft of her novel, *Save Me the Waltz*, while at the clinic.
June: Zelda discharged from clinic.

1933—*December*: Prohibition ends.

1934—*January*: Zelda has a third breakdown.
April: *Tender Is the Night* is published.

1935—Begins writing 'The Crack-Up' essays.

1936—Mother, Mollie Fitzgerald, dies.

1937—Moves to Hollywood to work as a screen-writer for MGM.
July: Meets Sheilah Graham.

1938—MGM contract not renewed.

1939—Takes on freelance writing assignments with various movie studios.
October: Begins work on *The Last Tycoon*.

1940—*January*: Publication of Pat Hobby stories begins in *Esquire*.
April: Zelda discharged from hospital; moves in with her mother in Montgomery.
December 21: Dies of heart attack at Sheilah Graham's apartment in Hollywood.

1941—*The Last Tycoon* is published.

1945—*The Crack-Up* is published.

1947—Zelda returns to psychiatric hospital.

1948—*March 10*: Zelda dies in fire at Highland Hospital, Asheville, North Carolina.

CHAPTER

NOTES

CHAPTER 1. THE JAZZ AGE

1. F. Scott Fitzgerald, *Tender Is the Night* (New York: Scribner's, 1995), p. 27.

2. Matthew J. Bruccoli, *Some Sort of Epic Grandeur: The Life of F. Scott Fitzgerald* (New York: Harcourt, Brace, and Jovanovich, 1981), p. 133.

3. "Authors on Fitzgerald," *F. Scott Fitzgerald's 100th Birthday*, n.d., <http://access.mpr.org/features/9609_fitzgerald/fitzauthors.htm> (May 20, 2003).

4. F. Scott Fitzgerald, *The Crack-Up* (New York: New Directions, 1956), p. 69.

5. F. Scott Fitzgerald, *Afternoon of an Author* (New York: Scribner's, 1957), p. 132.

6. Bryant Mangum, "F. Scott Fitzgerald," *Critical Survey of Long Fiction*, ed. Frank Magill (Hackensack, N.J.: Salem Press, Inc., 1981), p. 959.

7. "Authors on Fitzgerald."

8. F. Scott Fitzgerald, *This Side of Paradise* (New York: Signet Classic, 1996), p. 287.

CHAPTER 2. A ROMANTIC EGOTIST

1. Jeffrey Meyers, *Scott Fitzgerald: A Biography* (New York: HarperCollins, 1994), p. 11.

2. Ibid.

3. Matthew J. Bruccoli, *Some Sort of Epic Grandeur: The Life of F. Scott Fitzgerald* (New York: Harcourt, Brace, and Jovanovich, 1981), pp. 129–130.

4. Meyers, p. 17.

5. Bruccoli, p. 232.

6. Meyers, p. 22.

7. Ibid., p. 28.

8. Arthur Mizener, *Scott Fitzgerald and His World* (London: Thames and Hudson, 1972), p. 32.

9. Dinitia Smith, "Love Notes Drenched In Moonlight," *The New York Times*, September 8, 2003, p. E5.

10. James Mellow, *Invented Lives: F. Scott & Zelda Fitzgerald* (New York: Ballantine, 1984), p. 54.

11 Bruccoli, p. 93.

12. Ibid., p. 96.

13. Mellow, p. 63.

CHAPTER 3. A SUCCESSFUL DEBUT

1. *Correspondence of F. Scott Fitzgerald*, ed. Matthew J. Bruccoli *et al.* (New York: Random House, 1980), p. 55.

2. "The Victorian *Bildungsroman*," n.d., <http://www.stanford.edu/~steener/su02/english132/Bildungsroman.htm> (May 27, 2003).

3. James Mellow, *Invented Lives: F. Scott & Zelda Fitzgerald* (New York: Ballantine, 1984), p. 73.

CHAPTER 4. SELECTED SHORT STORIES

1. Matthew J. Bruccoli, *Some Sort of Epic Grandeur: The Life of F. Scott Fitzgerald* (New York: Harcourt, Brace, and Jovanovich, 1981), pp. 525–527.

2. F. Scott Fitzgerald, *Babylon Revisited* (New York: Scribner's, 1960), p. 10.

3. Ibid., p. 11.

4. Ibid., pp. 15–16.

5. Bruccoli, p. 110.

6. F. Scott Fitzgerald, "Bernice Bobs Her Hair," Collected Stories (New York: Scribner's, 1951), p. 48.

7. Ibid., p. 43.

8. Ibid., p. 47.

9. Ibid., p. 57.

10. Ibid., pp. 59–60.

CHAPTER 5. THE END OF INNOCENCE

1. F. Scott Fitzgerald, *The Beautiful and Damned* (New York: Scribner's, 1986), p. 8.

2. Ibid., pp. 111–112.

3. Ibid., p. 177.

4. F. Scott Fitzgerald, *Six Tales of the Jazz Age and Other Stories* (New York: Charles Scribner's Sons, 1960), p. 8.

5. *Correspondence of F. Scott Fitzgerald*, ed. Matthew J. Bruccoli *et al.* (New York: Random House, 1980), p. 600.

6. Fitzgerald, *The Beautiful and Damned*, p. 334.

7. Ibid., p. 334.

8. Ibid., p. 403.

9. Ibid., p. 447.

CHAPTER 6. SHATTERED DREAMS

1. *Correspondence of F. Scott Fitzgerald*, ed. Matthew J. Bruccoli *et al.* (New York: Random House, 1980), p. 68.

2. F. Scott Fitzgerald, *Babylon Revisited* (New York: Scribner's, 1960), p. 30.

3. Ibid., p. 35.

4. *The Great Gatsby: A Study*, ed. Frederick J. Hoffman (New York: Charles Scribner's Sons, 1962), pp. 245–254.

5. Fitzgerald, *Babylon Revisited*, p. 67.

6. Ibid., p. 75.

7. Ibid., p. 76.

8. Ibid., p. 81.

9. Ibid., p. 98.

10. Ibid., p. 99.

11. Ibid., p. 106.

12. *Correspondence of F. Scott Fitzgerald*, pp. 196–197.

CHAPTER 7. THE GREAT AMERICAN NOVEL

1. *Correspondence of F. Scott Fitzgerald*, ed. Matthew J. Bruccoli *et al.* (New York: Random House, 1980), p. 164.

2. F. Scott Fitzgerald, *The Great Gatsby* (New York: Scribner's, 1925), p. 23.

3. Ibid., p. 60.

4. Ibid., pp. 93–94.

5. Ibid., p. 99.

6. Ibid., p. 125.

7. *Twentieth Century Interpretations of The Great Gatsby*, ed. Ernest Lockridge (Englewood Cliffs, N.J.: Prentice-Hall, 1968), pp. 55–56.

8. Ibid.

9. F. Scott Fitzgerald, *The Great Gatsby* (New York: Scribner's, 1925), p. 160.

10. Kenneth Eble, *F. Scott Fitzgerald* (New York: Twayne, 1963), p. 93.

11. Ronald Berman, "The Great Gatsby and the Twenties," *The Cambridge Companion to F. Scott Fitzgerald* (Cambridge University Press, 2002), p. 94.

12. James W. Tuttleton, *The Novel of Manners in America* (Chapel Hill, N.C.: University of North Carolina Press, 1972), p. 68.

13. Eble, p. 91.

14. F. Scott Fitzgerald, *The Great Gatsby* (New York: Scribner's, 1925), p. 112.

CHAPTER 8. LOST AND WANDERING

1. *The Romantic Egoists*, ed. Matthew J. Bruccoli *et al.* (New York: Scribner's, 1974), p. 116.

2. F. Scott Fitzgerald, *The Crack-Up* (New York: New Directions, 1956), p. 125.

3. F. Scott Fitzgerald, *The Stories of F. Scott Fitzgerald* (New York: Charles Scribner's, 1951), p. 177.

4. Ibid., p. 208.

5. Matthew J. Bruccoli, *Some Sort of Epic Grandeur: The Life of F. Scott Fitzgerald* (New York: Harcourt, Brace, and Jovanovich, 1981), p. 258.

6. Jeffrey Meyers, *Scott Fitzgerald: A Biography* (New York: HarperCollins, 1994), p. 218.

CHAPTER 9. THE DARKEST NIGHT

1. Ernest Hemingway, *A Moveable Feast* (New York: Scribner's, 1964), p. 176.

2. Matthew J. Bruccoli, *Some Sort of Epic Grandeur: The Life of F. Scott Fitzgerald* (New York: Harcourt, Brace, and Jovanovich, 1981), p. 374.

3. *The Romantic Egoists*, ed. Matthew J. Bruccoli *et al.* (New York: Scribner's, 1974), p. 185.

4. Jeffrey Meyers, *Scott Fitzgerald: A Biography* (New York: HarperCollins, 1994), p. 264.

CHAPTER 10. LIFE AND LEGACY

1. Matthew J. Bruccoli, *Some Sort of Epic Grandeur: The Life of F. Scott Fitzgerald* (New York: Harcourt, Brace, and Jovanovich, 1981), p. 541.

2. Ibid., p. 471.

GLOSSARY

alliteration—The repetition of sounds in two or more neighboring words.

allusion—An incidental mention of something, designed to hint at some deeper meaning.

amalgam—A combination or mixture of different elements.

Babylon—An ancient city believed to be a place of excessive luxury and wickedness.

bildungsroman—A coming-of-age novel, generally concluding with the protagonist reaching maturity.

dichotomy—A division into two contradictory parts. In logic, a term used to describe the division of an idea in two, resulting in two new, opposite ideas.

epistolary—Contained or carried on by written correspondence; pertaining to or consisting of letters. An epistolary novel is a novel mainly consisting of letters written by the characters.

hedonism—A devotion to personal pleasure as a way of life; the doctrine that pleasure or happiness is the highest good.

irony—The use of words to express an idea that is opposite to the words' literal meaning.

juvenilia—A literary work written and designed for a young audience; also, works produced in a writer's youth.

literary device—A formula in writing for producing a certain effect, such as a figure of speech (a metaphor, for example), a narrative style (first person, third person, etc.), or a plot mechanism (such as a flashback).

mercenary—A soldier who fights for money; or, more generally, a person who works for the highest bidder with no other motivation than greed.

metaphor—A figure of speech in which a comparison is made between two words or phrases that have no literal relationship.

protagonist—The leading character or hero of a literary work.

roman à clef—A novel that represents historical events and characters under the guise of fiction.

socialism—A theory of social organization in which property, land, and means of production are communally owned rather than individually owned.

soliloquy—A literary character's speech made as if the person is alone. Often used in dramatic plays as a device to expose a character's private thoughts to the audience.

symbolism—The device of using one person or thing to represent or suggest another person or thing.

Major Works by F. Scott Fitzgerald

Novels:

This Side of Paradise (1920)
The Beautiful and Damned (1922)
The Great Gatsby (1924)
Tender Is the Night (1934)
The Last Tycoon (1945)

Short Story Collections:

Flappers and Philosophers (1920)
Tales of the Jazz Age (1922)
All the Sad Young Men (1926)
Taps At Reveille (1935)

Essays:

The Crack-Up (1945)
Afternoon of an Author (1957)

FURTHER READING

Bloom, Harold, ed. *F. Scott Fitzgerald: Comprehensive Research and Study Guide*. Broomall, Pa.: Chelsea House, 1999.

de Koster, Katie, ed. *Readings on F. Scott Fitzgerald*. San Diego, Calif.: Greenhaven Press, 1997.

Lazo, Caroline E. *F. Scott Fitzgerald: Voice of the Jazz Age*. Minneapolis, Minn.: The Lerner Publishing Group, 2003.

Pelzer, Linda C. *Student Companion to F. Scott Fitzgerald*. Westport, Conn.: Greenwood Press, 2000.

Stewart, Gail. *The Importance of F. Scott Fitzgerald*. Farmington Hills, Mich.: The Gale Group, 1999.

Tessitore, John. *F. Scott Fitzgerald: The American Dreamer*. Danbury, Conn.: Franklin Watts, 2001

INTERNET ADDRESSES

The F. Scott Fitzgerald Society Home Page
http://www.fitzgeraldsociety.org

F. Scott Fitzgerald Centenary Home Page
http://www.sc.edu/fitzgerald/

Internet Public Library—Online Literary Criticism Collection
http://www.ipl.org.ar/ref/litcrit/

INDEX